STAR
QUALTY
TALENT

Inspiring Hospitality Careers

STAR QUALITY TALENT

Inspiring Hospitality Careers

MONICA OR

RЗTHINK PRESS

First published in Great Britain 2018
by Rethink Press (www.rethinkpress.com)

WHAT OTHERS ARE SAYING ABOUT THE BOOK

The hospitality industry is filled with opportunities for everyone, whatever your background. Whether you are starting out as a kitchen porter, waiter, barman, chef or room attendant, the career stories within demonstrate how quickly you can progress and how the industry is proud to develop and nurture our star quality talent.

Passion, service and excellence go hand in hand to create promising careers for all. Monica's book is a must-read for anyone considering working in this vibrant, dynamic industry. Be inspired.

Fred Sirieix
General Manager, Galvin at Windows
***First Dates* Maître d', *Million Pound Menu* Host**

I have known Monica for many years; she is one of the most knowledgeable in her field and I feel honoured to have been asked to give a testimonial in this book. It is an easy read, with a clear path guiding you through the endless possibilities in a chosen career in the hospitality sector, and indeed the star quality needed to be a success in embracing your natural talent. I am lucky to have worked with some of these talents and seen them progress through the ranks and gain immense satisfaction from their role in this beautiful industry, which is also one of the largest employment sectors in the UK. I trust that all who read it get as much insight, enlightenment and joy in reading it as I did.

Daniel Ayton BA (Hons) FIH
President of the Disciples Escoffier UK
Senior Vice-President, World Master Chefs Society

A great read! A fascinating insight into some very personal and inspiring journeys by iconic hospitality professionals, coupled with extremely practical advice for all practitioners (not just those entering the industry!). Monica continues to delight and inform, and proves herself once again to be closely connected and empathetic to the industry she most obviously loves.

Paul Evans FIH
Chair, Institute of Hospitality, London
Hospitality professional at Consultinc Ltd

After twenty-five years of upskilling staff in the hospitality sector, I found this book extremely useful and relevant for anyone in the industry.

Monica draws on her vast knowledge and insightful case studies to produce an inspirational and practical book, ideal for new staff, but also beneficial for those with existing hospitality experience.

Upskill People is privileged to have drawn on Monica's experience for some of our e-learning content and I'm sure you'll find the book as insightful as I did. If more people followed the book's advice and tips, I'm certain the industry would be facing fewer of the recruitment struggles it currently does.

Pete Fullard
Managing Director, Upskill People

A good inspirational read for talent joining the hospitality industry, with some excellent examples of success. It clearly demonstrates that with hard work and vision you can succeed. Always rise to a challenge: with a great attitude and determined vision you will achieve your goal.

Debrah Dugga
Managing Director, Dukes Hotel

Monica has really shown how amazing careers in hospitality can be, from the excitement of the industry to the travel that you can do. Not only is this book a great insight into careers within hospitality but it is also packed full of really useful careers information, advice and guidance for everyone to be able to learn something new. This is a must-read book, whether you are someone just starting your career or an experienced professional. It's your guidebook to your career and it should never be that far away from you.

Sam Coulstock, FIH
Business Relations Director, Umbrella Training

Monica's latest book provides a series of fascinating case studies that perfectly illustrate the breadth of opportunity and variety that a career in hospitality can provide. Monica's own career has been very varied. As readers, we are lucky that, among her many talents, she has a gift for passing on her knowledge and expertise in prose that is engaging, concise and crystal clear. This book does an excellent job in promoting our industry and showing new entrants the path to fulfilment and success.

Ben Walker, MIH
Editor, *HQ Magazine*

CONTENTS

FOREWORD

As one who has built his life and career within what I feel is the greatest industry in the world, I feel very strongly about the high-handed approach other industries have about hospitality and how they often feel that it is designed to suit failures in life. Parents, teachers, careers advisors, government ministers and bodies have forever dissuaded young people from venturing into what transpires to be the greatest industry in the world.

For me, no other industry in the world offers as much scope and development – both personally and vocationally – breadth and width of career opportunities, and the possibility to dream of successes beyond one's imagination.

A warrior who has been promoting the image of my industry for as long as I can remember, Monica Or brings yet another breath of fresh air to my thinking with this book. Why, for God's sake, have we never thought of a book like this? This is a people's industry, built by people, for people.

When the industry is always struggling to recruit new talent, to nurture them to grow and to succeed, why has it never published a book like this before? It speaks out, in fact shouts, to the young blood out there awaiting a fabulous career, saying, 'Here, read me, look at me and try me out, for I can promise you a career of hope, prosperity and successes beyond your wildest dreams.'

I am thrilled that Monica has put pen to paper and brought this book about, which I hope inspires the youth, the adults, the retired and the aspiring to grasp a little about the many doors and avenues within our great industry that lie open and awaiting the right person all the time.

This industry may be tough at times, hard at times, frustrating at times, angering at times, trying your patience many a time. BUT this is the industry that, without making any promises, promises that it will lead you on a journey beyond your wildest dreams, with career prospects that can only be driven by you and your will to succeed. When that combination comes alive, the sky may be too close to reach and achieve your ambitions.

The success stories in our industry go beyond any other and it simply shows that this industry seeks not big degrees, high IQ, super-intelligence... All it wants from you is that you should be human and industrious, hard-working – and have focus. Age and colour, education and qualification are no barriers here. Success is purely personal, achievements are hugely appreciated, and making bonds and friendships are true examples of the human spirit of family and togetherness.

I hope this book goes on to make massive waves and I wish that every hospitality tutor, college, institute, industry body and association would get together and tell every young aspiring individual to read this book and let it open in their minds a real gusto and spirit of adventure, and encourage them all to aspire to reach those goals that they should aspire to reach.

My thanks to Monica for playing the trump card!

All the very best and my sincerest wishes to all those who read this book and achieve their dreams.

Cyrus Todiwala, OBE DL
Chef Proprietor, *Café Spice Namaste*
Celebrity chef on *Saturday Kitchen* **and**
The Incredible Spice Men

INTRODUCTION: GETTING STARTED

Welcome to the world of hospitality: a world full of opportunities, a world full of possibilities. If you are looking to embark on a career in hospitality or looking for a career change, then you have come to the right place.

This book will show you how vast the hospitality industry is. I will share with you the career stories of those currently working in our industry, including my own. I will give you top tips on how to start or to progress your career within hospitality, looking at the different options available. I will also introduce to you some of the many organisations that can help you throughout your career journey.

The hospitality industry is the fourth largest industry in the United Kingdom. According to the British Hospitality Association (now known as UKHospitality), in 2017 the hospitality industry accounted for 2.6 million jobs through direct employment, and by 2021 an additional 518,000 staff will be needed. The industry spans fourteen sectors:

- Hotels

- Restaurants

- Pubs, bars and nightclubs

- Gambling

- Members' clubs

- Hostels

- Food services (formerly known as contract catering, which is outsourced)

- Holiday parks

- Self-catering

- Visitor attractions

- Tourist services

- Travel services

- Events

- Hospitality services (these are services managed in-house)

If you have ever wondered what it is like to work in the hospitality industry, and if you think it is an industry that could offer you a great career, then let me share my story with you.

Like many teenagers, when I was at school I really did not know what I wanted to do or where my first job would lead me – until I read the book *Hotel*, by Arthur Hailey. It is set in the St Gregory Hotel in New Orleans, and the story follows the management of this independent hotel as it struggles to remain profitable and avoid being taken over by a chain hotel. The book reveals what happens behind the scenes of glitz and glamour, and through it I gained my first insights into what it could be like to work in a luxury hotel.

This bestselling novel was turned into a film in 1967, and in 1983 it was adapted into a television series, in which the hotel was based in San Francisco. The front of the Fairmont Hotel in San Francisco was famously featured in the filming of the series.

Having read this book, I knew that I wanted to work in a hotel. But how do you go about it?

I was keen to get some experience. Like many parents, mine had aspirations for me to become a doctor, lawyer or accountant. I was adamant that this was not the career route for me, so they supported me the best way they could. They had no knowledge of the industry, but they helped me get a Saturday job working in the dispense bar (the area where drinks are prepared for diners) of a Chinese restaurant. This was not quite what I had in mind. I think they were secretly hoping this experience would dissuade me from pursuing my dreams of working in a hotel. As I was still at school I was not allowed to serve alcohol, so I could only pour soft drinks and make coffee in the bar, but I guess we all have to start somewhere. This really was not the experience I was after, though, and needless to say I did not stay long. However, I kept my sights on the goal of working in a luxury hotel. I just had to figure out a better way to get there.

I spoke to my careers advisor at school and we looked at catering colleges. I had also heard about Springboard, which gives careers advice to those interested in working in hospitality, leisure and tourism. I remember going to their offices, but being a very shy teenager I carried on walking and never went in. However, later in my life our paths would cross once more, in a very different way.

I carried on at school, taking the traditional route of GCSEs and A-Levels, not really knowing what other options there were at the time. I was not particularly focused on academia, and when my A-Level results came through it was no surprise that I did not get the A-Levels, let alone the grades, for any of the universities I had applied for.

I remember looking through the newspaper at adverts for colleges and universities and saw one for South Devon College, which was offering a hotel management course. I called them and moved from London to Torquay the next day. I lived, worked and studied there for the next three years – my hospitality journey had truly begun.

During those three years I learned so much and gained my food hygiene certificate, wine and spirit education trust certificate, chef and train-the-trainer qualifications, and a hotel management qualification. In those days this gave me automatic affiliation to the Hotel Catering Institutional Management Association (HCIMA), which is now known as the Institute of Hospitality.

I was also determined to get as much practical experience as I could. I worked in several of the hotels in Torquay: the most memorable for me was a three-star, independently-run hotel, where I worked on reception and in the bar. Whenever I was on a late shift, I worked in the bar and the owner would come down and order his Tio Pepe, which was to be served in a wine glass with one ice cube. He was very particular about how he wanted this served. The then manager was a recovering alcoholic, and we had some interesting times working together in the hotel.

I was also a student member of the HCIMA, Devon and Cornwall branch, and was involved in organising student events. Little did I know that some twenty years later I would become chair of the London branch for the Institute of Hospitality.

While at college I had a fleeting moment when I considered joining the Army Catering Corps. My chef lecturer ran army camps in the summer and took some of his students with him. When I asked if I could go along, he diplomatically said no, although to make up for this he gave me a job at one of his private catering events. Later on in my career, I did end up working with the British Army, but more about that later.

On my hotel management course I had to undertake two industry placements, and I knew that this would be my opportunity to work in a five-star luxury hotel. I decided to organise my own placements as I wanted to return to London, and I wrote to all the top London hotels. I had my first placement at the Ritz, working in the housekeeping department. During my time there, I worked in the linen room, cleaned bedrooms and worked as a housekeeping supervisor.

I was to do my second placement at the end of my college course, and I was determined to apply for a full-time job and use this as part of my placement experience. I worked at the Vanderbilt Hotel, part of the Edwardian Group, in reservations and had some great training there, working alongside the lovely Dorothy, also fondly known as 'the lady in the comfortable shoes'. For successfully organising these placements I was awarded the Karen Littlejohns trophy for Best Work Placement Student.

I worked for Edwardian Hotels for several years, at the Vanderbilt and the Grafton, working my way up to reservations supervisor and then moving on to personnel. During my time there, the hotel group went through business

process re-engineering – an early 1990s business strategy –
and became Radisson Edwardian.

It was at this point that I grew a little restless and wanted
to broaden my experience. I wanted to gain international
experience. A few years earlier, when I was on holiday with
my parents, I was fortunate enough to go on a short cruise
on the *Queen Elizabeth 2* (*QE2*) ship. I'd made a point of
meeting the hotel manager so I could find out some more
about working on a luxury cruise liner. I had a meeting with
Mr John Duffy, and he organised a private tour for me of the
back-of-house hotel areas. I knew then that one day I would
work on a cruise ship, although I had no idea that I would
end up working for him.

The time had come for that new adventure. I wrote to
Cunard and applied to join their fleet. I was appointed as
4th purser on the Cunard *Countess*, which was based in
the Caribbean. For me this was a dream come true. Now,
if you are wondering what exactly a 4th purser does, it is
the equivalent of working in a hotel reception, as they hold
the 'purse strings' on the ship. The *Countess* was a small ship
and the hotel manager was very self-sufficient. When he
was on leave a relief hotel manager would come on board.
It just so happened that the relief hotel manager was also
the relief hotel manager on the *QE2*. Coming from a much
larger ship, he was used to having his own secretary. Being
the helpful person that I am, I volunteered to carry out his

secretarial work, not thinking anything of taking on these extra duties.

A few months later, I heard that Cunard was looking to sell the *Countess*. I was in my early twenties and did not want to get made redundant, so I wrote to the head office and asked for a transfer. After being recommended by the relief hotel manager I was transferred to the *QE2* and was the hotel manager's secretary, working for the legendary John Duffy. The late John Duffy worked for Cunard for forty-seven years and was their youngest hotel manager at the age of thirty-three. He was the longest serving hotel manager on the *QE2*, and then he was hotel manager on the *Queen Mary 2* before retiring.

I thoroughly enjoyed my time working on the cruise ships, but eventually it was time to go back shoreside. I returned to London and worked for Fortissimo, a division of Berkeley Scott, recruiting for all of Forte's Hotels in London. Wanting to further my education, and now realising that my passion in hospitality was focused on the staff, I studied for a master's degree in personnel management in Bristol.

This was the hardest year of my life. Remember I said I was not very academic at school, so studying for a master's degree was a huge undertaking for me. It was only later in life that I realised why I struggled so much. I was assessed as being mildly dyslexic. As an adult I developed strategies to cope, and I hid it well so it was never detected. Through blood, sweat and tears I came out the other end and qualified as a member of the Chartered Institute of Personnel and Development (CIPD).

I then returned to London and worked as a human resource manager for Hilton Hotels. This is where my path with Springboard crossed once more, when I was interviewed and featured in one of their career magazines.

I joined Hilton at the time it took over Stakis Hotels and was involved in the changeover process of their systems and procedures. I worked in five of their London hotels, opened the Hilton London Trafalgar, was involved in the refurbishment of the Hilton London Green Park, was cluster human resource manager for several of their London hotels and ended up looking after the training delivery for the London region.

I knew at this point that training and development was my true passion. I returned to education once more and studied for my Postgraduate Certificate in Education (PGCE) and worked at Westminster Kingsway College as a higher education lecturer on its hospitality management degree courses.

It was during my time at Westminster Kingsway College that I looked after hospitality employer groups. I taught Travelodge hotel managers on a blended learning basis and army students from the Royal Logistic Corps through distance learning. I became a dab hand at writing and developing e-learning courses and managing students online. This was no mean feat, particularly as my army cohorts were posted all over the world, including Afghanistan and Kenya.

I was also keen to engage with industry employers and that is how I got invited to join the Institute of Hospitality London Branch. From starting off as the education liaison officer, I was elected as vice-chair and subsequently became chair for London – the only female chair that the Institute of Hospitality has had for London to date.

After working in hotels, gaining international experience on cruise ships, being involved in the processes of hotel take-overs, openings and refurbishments, working in education and chairing the Institute of Hospitality, London, I decided it was time to bring all of these experiences together. I started my own consultancy company, Star Quality Hospitality Consultancy, which specialises in working operationally with independent hotels and restaurants, focusing on the guest experience.

My story is very much focused on hotels, but there are fourteen different sectors that you could work in. The beauty of the hospitality industry is that it is easy to move from one sector to another if you wish to, as the skills you will learn are transferable.

This book is divided into three sections. The first section will look at the inspiring career stories of people who work in the industry, to give you an idea of its scope and scale. At the end of each career story there is a link to the full video interview that was carried out with these hospitality professionals.

The second section will give you top tips and advice on how to get a job in hospitality, unveiling some of the tools that recruiters use but don't tell you about. The focus is very much on the soft skills, attitude, behaviour and social interaction that are expected of people working in this industry.

The third section will look at the training, support and guidance available to you throughout your hospitality career. Again, there are video links to interviews that were carried out with these organisations and these go into more detail about how they can help you. Feel free to dip in and out of the sections that are most relevant to you.

This book focuses on the UK market. However, the hospitality industry is international and you will see that there are plenty of ways to expand your experience across the globe.

SECTION 1

INSPIRING HOSPITALITY
CAREER STORIES

In this section we will look at a range of hospitality career stories – specifically at each individual's journey, from how they started out their first job in hospitality to how they got to where they are now. All of these hospitality professionals have taken different routes and worked in different job roles and sectors of the industry. This will give you an idea of the opportunities available within hospitality and give you an insight into what you could do and how far you could go with your own career.

At the end of each person's career story there is a video link, which will show the full interview as they describe in their own words why they chose to work in hospitality.

From family firm to becoming the youngest member of the Golden Keys Society

Jack McCarthy is currently the deputy head concierge at The Cavendish in London and has already won three prestigious industry awards. His family was expecting him to work in their building firm after he left school, but at the age of 14, Jack was lucky enough to get a taste of hotel life when he did some work experience at The Cavendish hotel in London. He was fascinated by the amount of trust guests place with the concierge and the many opportunities he had to leave a lasting impression. He was attracted to the role of concierge because every day was different and he constantly faced new challenges.

After leaving school at the young age of 16, Jack started working at the Savoy Hotel as a concierge assistant. After two promotions there, he made the move to join the concierge team at Brown's Hotel in Mayfair before joining The Cavendish, deputising for the head concierge. This move gave him greater responsibility and the chance to develop his own management style.

Jack was awarded Concierge of the Year at the Boutique Hotelier Awards in 2016, and in 2017 he became the youngest member of the prestigious Les Clefs d'Or Society. Jack says: 'Since starting my career in hospitality I have always looked up to the experienced concierges who wear the golden keys on their lapels. It is an honour to be part of the society.'

After his interview, Jack also became one of the winners of the 2018 Acorn Awards, an accolade awarded annually to 30 aspiring individuals under the age of 30.

Advice from Jack McCarthy: 'If you have a natural charisma with people and you enjoy dealing with people, these are the fundamentals that you need to go into the hospitality industry. If you have got that passion and drive, it might be that everything else can be taught on the job.'

The full video interview with Jack McCarthy can be watched on this link:

www.vimeo.com/264485039

From B&B to award-winning tour guide

Alex Graeme runs Unique Devon Tours, which has established an outstanding reputation as an award-winning tour guide company. It has won gold for three consecutive years at the prestigious Visit Devon Tourism Awards and gold at the South Devon and English Riviera Tourism Awards. Alex has also been ranked as one of the top eight tour guides globally in *Wanderlust* travel magazine's World Guide of the Year Awards.

Alex's hospitality career began when he was a child, cleaning bedrooms to earn some pocket money at his parents' bed and breakfast. Not really knowing what he wanted to do, he went to college and studied hotel management, although at the back of his mind he dreamed of being a tour guide.

Alex worked in numerous jobs, both in and out of hospitality. For a while he worked in the care industry and in social services, but did not feel fulfilled and knew there was something more he could be doing. He set his sights on revisiting his pipe dream of being a tour guide and turning it into a reality. That is when Unique Devon Tours was born.

In the short time that Alex has run his company, he has become the go-to tour guide in Devon. His featured tours are the Hound of the Baskervilles and the Agatha Christie tours and he is a huge hit with the American market.

Alex's dream is to put Devon well and truly on the map as the place to visit.

Advice from Alex Graeme: 'Play to your strengths. If you can match your natural skills, the ones you are born with, to a career, then you have got a very good chance of succeeding. You also have to put your heart into it. Love what you do.'

The full video interview with Alex Graeme can be watched on this link:

www.vimeo.com/266290206

From medical aspirations to becoming a hotel general manager

Arun Kumar is currently the general manager of the Sunborn Yacht Hotel in London. When he was younger he dreamed of being a medical doctor and was strongly encouraged by his parents. However, as he puts it, 'I did not fancy the hospital smell, so I had to do something different.'

This was the turning point in his life. He studied hotel management at the Institute of Hotel Management in India and had an internship with the Sheraton Group, starting off as a room service waiter.

Taking a traditional route, Arun worked in various departments and moved up the ranks to supervisor, assistant manager, deputy manager and finally general manager. He has been involved in many different hotel projects, including building conversions, refurbishments and hotel openings in London.

Arun is extremely passionate about the hotel industry. 'It started purely from curiosity. Working in hospitality is like living a new life every day... Given an opportunity, it is all in our hands... This industry is unique. You deal with people, you deal with emotions, you deal with so many things you cannot predict,' he says.

> **Advice from Arun Kumar**: 'If you want to feel energy, if you want to keep motivated and you want to be challenged, this is the right industry. If you get a chance to work in this industry, you are one of the lucky ones. Never turn it down. It is not easy, I can give you that, but it is worth it.'

The full video interview with Arun Kumar can be watched on this link:

www.vimeo.com/264482800

From waitress to Royal Household uniform designer

Katie Young Gerald is the owner of Bespoke Textiles, a fashion supplier that works closely with the hospitality industry, bringing style to unique uniforms, people and places.

Like many people, Katie started working in the hospitality industry as a waitress during her summer holidays when she was at school, and to get her through university. Katie studied fashion textiles and has worked for some famous fashion brands, including Betty Jackson. She relocated to Hong Kong and went on to build her own global manufacturing company.

Now back in London, Katie works with hospitality brands designing bespoke items, from napkins, aprons, t-shirts and bags through to full uniforms. She works with some of the leading hospitality companies such as Soho House, The Ivy and even the Royal Household.

Advice from Katie Young Gerald: 'I would say you have got to be a people person to work in this industry. If you love people and you love food, and the dynamic environment hospitality typically has, then this is the industry for you. There are so many ways to work with hospitality, whether it is marketing, service, or being a host.'

The full video interview with Katie Young Gerald can be watched on this link:

www.vimeo.com/266382052

From housekeeping to human resource manager

Anna Napora came from Poland to London with no qualifications or experience and could barely speak English. She started working at The Landmark London as a room attendant and banqueting assistant. Some 16 years later, still at The Landmark London, Anna is now the human resource manager.

Anna relays her story of how she progressed through a variety of positions – from housekeeping, to food and beverage to human resources; how she managed seven different departments, got promoted numerous times, and how she combined work and study to further her knowledge of hospitality.

She studied for her BA in hospitality management at Westminster Kingsway College while working full time at The Landmark London in the bar. Working until 4am, Anna would then go to college for 8am, and continued to do this for the three years of her studies. After several promotions she moved to human resources and once again studied, this time for her Chartered Institute of Personnel and Development qualification.

Anna says she has been fortunate that the managers that she has worked with have spotted her potential and given her opportunities to further her career while at The Landmark London.

> **Advice from Anna Napora**: 'Hospitality is not for every-one, it is a challenging industry, but it is quite rewarding. You need to have hospitality within you; if you don't have it, then you are not the right person... I think sometimes people struggle to understand that we are here to serve others. As long as you are willing to learn and you have the right attitude and behaviour, that already is a lot.'

The full video interview with Anna Napora can be watched on this link:

www.vimeo.com/265262976

From gardener to managing director of a country house hotel

Mark Godfrey is the managing director of the Deer Park Country House Hotel in Honiton, Devon. He was origi-nally on a youth training scheme to become a gardener, and took a loan from his dad to buy a motorbike so he could get to his workplace. To earn some extra money to pay his dad back he started working as a pot wash in the kitchen of his local golf club and says the camaraderie and teamwork that he experienced behind the scenes opened his eyes to the world of hospitality.

He went on to study hotel management at Bournemouth College, and during his time there gained experience from working in a two-Michelin-starred restaurant in Paris. He took on a trainee management role at the Dormy Hotel and also worked at The Grand in Brighton, which was owned by De Vere Hotels at the time. Mark was involved in hotel openings while working with De Vere Hotels and took his first general management role at the age of twenty-six at Alexander House in West Sussex.

He also worked at the Dart Marina after relocating to Devon. After eight years there, the owner gave him and his partner two round-the-world business class seats to travel the world. He returned a year later and became the managing director for Harbour Hotels.

Mark now runs a hospitality consultancy and one of his clients, Deer Park Hotel, asked him to join as their managing director and part owner. Mark is also a Master Innholder and a member of the South West Board for Hospitality Action.

Advice from Mark Godfrey: 'Just do it. There are 131 different careers in hospitality. Even if you want to be an accountant, go niche. Be an accountant in the hospitality industry. Be the best you can. Hospitality has a career for everybody and you can work all over the world. Don't miss a career of a lifetime. Join hospitality.'

The full video interview with Mark Godfrey can be watched on this link:

www.vimeo.com/266259189

From civil engineer to fine dining chef

Grant Ridley is a qualified civil engineer from Australia with a degree in engineering and currently works at the Sea Containers Restaurant at the Mondrion London as a chef.

During his career, Grant has been involved in large projects around the world, building bridges and sky scrapers. He was also involved in the T5 project at Heathrow for three and a half years. His two passions outside of this were cooking and travelling.

While in London, Grant fell on some hard times and went through a divorce. During this time, he came across the Beyond Food Foundation, a social enterprise set up by Simon Boyle, who runs chef apprenticeships at The Brigade Bar and Bistro at London Bridge (you can read more about this in the third section of the book).

Grant joined The Brigade as an apprentice chef, fast-tracked his way through this and is now working at the fine dining Sea Containers Restaurant. Grant hopes to combine his engineering skills with his passion for food and to build on his career as a chef. As he says, 'I am too old to be a builder; hopefully I am not too old to be a chef.'

Grant says that people are polite and they thank him for the food, but what he loves most is 'When you hear those comments "oh that was fantastic" and they don't know you are actually standing round the corner. That's nice, that's where the rewards are.'

> **Advice from Grant Ridley**: 'Follow what you love, the learning curve is steep. It is all-consuming. Since the day I started I threw myself 100% into it. You are doing something you love with people who share the same passion as you, so you don't want to be late. You want to get there, you want to learn and you want to produce.'

When I interviewed Grant he was about to cook a meal for forty-five people at one of Simon Boyle's Social Diner Supper Club events.

The full video interview with Grant Ridley can be watched on this link:

www.vimeo.com/266349968

From home cooking to golf and country club manager

Chris Jones is currently the manager of the Exeter Golf and Country Club. His passion for the industry was ignited through his love of cooking. He used to cook with his mum as a young child and his dream was to run his own restaurant. When he was at school he spoke to his career advisor and was advised to study hotel management, as he could get both cheffing and management experience on the course. After studying at college, his work experience moved him more front-of-house, and he pursued a career in management.

He gained all-round, hands-on experience working in three-star hotels in Torquay. His big break came when he worked at the Palace Hotel under Master Innholder Paul Uphill. Chris has managed the Dart Marina Hotel, transforming it from a three-star to a four-star hotel with a two-AA-Rosette restaurant. Even though he was made redundant, his love of the industry spurred him on and he is now successfully managing the Exeter Golf and Country Club. The increase in revenue that has been generated under his management means money can be reinvested back into the club to continually improve it as it goes from strength to strength.

> **Advice from Chris Jones**: 'Work hard, play hard as well. Enjoy it, it is a fun industry to be in.'

The full video interview with Chris Jones can be watched on this link:

www.vimeo.com/266310640

From serving hospital meals to chairing the NACC

Neel Radia has had a varied career in and out of hospitality, and has won numerous industry awards. He is currently the regional account executive with Brakes Group, a supplier to the food service sector. He is also the chair of the National Association of Care Catering (NACC).

Neel has always had a passion for food and studied for a GNVQ at college in hospitality management, an advanced GNVQ in tourism management, and then completed his

BA (Hons) degree in tourism management at Brighton University. During his summer holidays he worked at Bupa, serving meals to patients.

After he graduated, Neel moved to America and worked at the Epcot Centre in Walt Disney World Resort in Florida as a cultural representative. He then returned to the UK and worked in retail for a few years before backpacking around Australia, New Zealand and South East Asia. During his travels he worked in hotels and restaurants as he was on a working holiday visa.

When he returned once more to the UK he worked for a food manufacturing company called Raj Foods for thirteen years and volunteered in his spare time with food-related charities.

One of the charities is the NACC, and he is currently their national chair. The latest project he was been working on is one of his biggest achievements to date: setting up a Level 2 qualification in health and social care catering, specifically for chefs working in the healthcare sector. This is the first qualification of its kind to be introduced to colleges.

Neel has also been recognised with some prestigious industry awards. In 2015, he won a Catey Award for going the extra mile in food service. In 2017, he was named Public Sector Caterer of the Year and also picked up the marketing award for the Meals on Wheels campaign he has been running for the last four years.

Since being interviewed Neel has won another Catey and was named Public Sector Caterer of the Year once again in 2018.

> **Advice from Neel Radia:** 'My advice for anyone coming to this sector is please do. It is a brilliant sector to work in. People always see hospitality as a Cinderella kind of service – absolutely wrong! There are so many opportunities, whether you are interested in the chef side or the management side. There are many different career paths you can take. It is a fun industry to work in, and the rewards are great.'

The full video interview with Neel Radia can be watched on this link:

www.vimeo.com/267301722

From pot wash to guest relations manager by the age of 21

Mitchell Collier is the guest relations manager at Belmond Le Manoir aux Quat'Saison in Oxford, a hotel whose chef patron is Raymond Blanc. Mitchell was promoted to the role at the age of twenty-one and is the youngest guest relations manager ever to be employed there.

Mitchell's original dream was to become a pastry chef and he worked as a pot wash to earn some pocket money before studying hospitality management at Derby University. It was during his studies that he became interested in the front-of-house side of the industry and decided to focus his career in this area.

Mitchell worked with esteemed hotelier Danny Pecorelli at South Lodge Hotel in West Sussex before moving to Le Manoir. A driven individual, Mitchell is always looking for his next achievement. He says, 'Working around such incredible people helps drive that inspiration and desire to get to the next level'.

Things have not always been smooth sailing for him, however. As he was about to turn twenty-one, his health rapidly declined and Mitchell was rushed to hospital for emergency surgery. After having some tests he was diagnosed with cancer. During this time, he was unsuccessful with an internal promotion he had applied for and his relationship with his girlfriend ended. Usually a positive and happy person, this series of events knocked him, as it would anyone.

The silver lining came when he was told about the work of Hospitality Action, the industry's benevolent organisation that helps people who work, or have worked, in hospitality and are in crisis (you can read more about their work in the third section of this book). Mitchell contacted them and he was given counselling to help him through this period. Then in November 2017, he was given the all-clear from cancer, was promoted to guest relations manager at Le Manoir, and a month later embarked on a new relationship.

Mitchell says, 'Hospitality is a challenging industry but in a good way. It constantly requires the best from you, because you are not only doing it for yourself – you are doing it for your guests or clients. In a sense, your success is their success.'

> **Advice from Mitchell Collier**: 'Always have that next objective; there is always something that you can keep pushing yourself for. "Shoot for the stars because even if you miss you are out of this world." This is a great thing to keep in mind and is relevant to what we do here in hospitality. It is a fantastic industry; you will make friends for life, and you will have memories for life as well.'

The full video interview with Mitchell Collier can be watched on this link:

www.vimeo.com/269840542

From family inspiration to becoming a development chef

Rhys Richardson works as a senior development chef with Servest, a facilities management company in the UK. He says he was inspired by his family, who were working in the hospitality industry, and decided to train as a chef. It was his grandmother who gave him some great advice, which Rhys shares: 'If you choose to go into hospitality, you will always have a job.'

After he finished school Rhys took a traditional route and went to college to train as a chef. His work experience at a big city law firm helped to get him his first job as a commis chef, working for a contract catering company.

He moved into restaurants for a short time to broaden his experience and worked for Marcus Wareing at Petrus, gaining Michelin star experience. He soon realised, however, that the restaurant environment was not what he wanted and he moved backed to contract catering, where he has established his career.

Working with Baxter Storey, Rhys has run large catering functions, from buffet and canape events through to private dining. Rhys has worked in many different establishments through his contract catering work, including Barclays' world headquarters. He also opened Goldman Sachs on Fleet Street, serving high-end clients in a Michelin-star-equivalent dining environment.

Rhys wanted to further his qualifications and went to Westminster Kingsway College to study for a foundation degree in culinary arts. It was after this that he made the move to become a development chef, working with Harbour and Jones and then Servest. At Servest, Rhys has been developing new brands and mentoring chefs within the organisation. He was the lead in setting up and establishing the culinary classroom.

> **Advice from Rhys Richardson**: 'You need to be focused and determined and you need to come into the industry with a clear goal of what you want to achieve. Join the hospitality industry, get experience, go through the ranks and meet as many people as you can. Network as much as you can and just be really open minded. It is a great industry to be a part of and you can build a fantastic career in hospitality.'

The full video interview with Rhys Richardson can be watched on this link:

www.vimeo.com/271858980

From working at a theme park to running large corporate events

Philip Berners currently works at The Edge Hotel School where he shares his vast experience of event management with students studying for their Bachelor of Arts degrees in hotel management and events management.

Philip's career in hospitality started when he got a work placement at Thorpe Park, where he gained experience in recruitment and training and supervising the cleaning. He was then offered a full-time position as head of events organising corporate events, days out and VIP arrivals.

His event management career took off when he worked at The London Hippodrome, which at the time was a night-club but has since been turned into a casino. He managed a further eight venues, organising events and bookings with this company, after which he worked for Marco Pierre White looking after the Sugar Reef and Little Havana restaurants in London.

He later went on to set up his own event management company and was involved in a worldwide album launch for Bon Jovi. He has also worked with Shania Twain and Jennifer Lopez. For three years he was a senior manager for the Brit Awards, and he can count the Queen as one of his previous clients, after he organised a party she was hosting in Windsor Great Park.

Philip then moved back to Poland for ten years, where he continued organising events. When he returned to England he went into teaching and is now at The Edge Hotel School in Colchester.

Advice from Philip Berners: 'Get out into a hotel, work at an event, get some knowledge and experience and network with people. In the hospitality and tourism industry, events are closely linked; people know each other and it is important to network. If you are thinking of working in hospitality, network, get experience and if you can get a qualification that will help you.'

The full video interview with Philip Berners can be watched on this link:

www.vimeo.com/272926825

From studying economics to becoming an executive housekeeper

Sebastian Dabrowski has worked in the hospitality industry for more than seventeen years. While at school in Poland he studied for a diploma in economics and accounting, although he has never worked in this profession.

After working as a waiter in Poland he decided that the hospitality industry was where he wanted to be as he loved serving others and helping customers. An opportunity arose to work on cruise ships and he left his native country to work on board ships for seven years. He worked for several companies, including Cunard, and during this time his management potential was spotted and he was trained up as an assistant housekeeper.

Sebastian reveals, 'I never knew what housekeeping was until I started to work in this department.'

By the time he was twenty-five he was an executive house-keeper. After travelling the world and gaining a wealth of experience on cruise ships, Sebastian decided to settle in the UK. He worked as an executive housekeeper for some prestigious hotels in London, including the Ritz London, The Connaught and Brown's Hotel.

Sebastian says, 'Throughout my career in hospitality, one thing I have to highlight is the amount of training and development that I went through. It is an amazing industry and it is an amazing career, where you can learn not only about the job itself, but the transferable skills you can use somewhere else.'

Sebastian has also been nominated as Housekeeper of the Year in the Hotel Catey Awards, which is often compared to winning an Oscar in hospitality. He also holds a senior role with the United Kingdom Housekeeping Association (UKHA – you can read more about their work in the third section of this book). His work at The Connaught hotel helped it to gain a five-star Forbes rating – the first hotel in London to achieve this accolade.

> **Advice from Sebastian Dabrowski**: 'It is hard work, I can promise you that, but you learn a lot at the same time. The experience is worth it. You meet some incredible people and you work with some incredible people. You work for some incredible properties and you can achieve so much. A career in hospitality always starts at the bottom, but if you have the passion for hospitality and like working with people then your career can rise very quickly.'

The full video interview with Sebastian Dabrowski can be watched on this link:

www.vimeo.com/273508209

From barman to general manager of a backpacker's hostel

Stuart Ball is the general manager of SoHostel, a backpacker's hostel in Soho, London. Stuart started his career working behind the bar in a local pub and that was where his interest in hospitality began. He loves interacting with people, meeting people from different places and learning about their expectations. In his interview he discusses the satisfaction he feels when customers leave at the end of the evening having had a good time.

Stuart continued to work in pubs, was promoted and quickly became the landlord of his own pub in Kent in his mid twenties. He says he enjoyed serving the local community for several years as a pub landlord.

After taking a career break from the hospitality industry, Stuart eventually moved back to London and spent a lot of time working with homeless people on the streets of Soho. It was this work that led him to become involved in the design and development of SoHostel.

SoHostel was originally a 175-bed backpackers' hostel when it opened in November 2013. It has now expanded to 295 beds and has a small restaurant, café and two licensed bars, one of which is a roof top bar.

After working on the design and development of SoHostel, Stuart became the general manager of the property. The hostel has proved to be very popular. To cope with the demand, it was expanded a few years later and continues to thrive.

> **Advice from Stuart Ball**: 'Every day is different and every day will bring you fresh challenges. People think it will be easy, but it is hard work. However, if you put the hard work in, the rewards are there to be gained. Employers are always looking for good, committed staff and the pace of progression can be quite quick if you put the work in.'

The full video interview with Stuart Ball can be watched on this link:

www.vimeo.com/273724554

From the personal stories above you can see how a passion for serving people has spurred these individuals on to develop careers in this vibrant industry. By gaining experience in different organisations and furthering their knowledge through training and education they have all pursued fulfilling careers.

There is a famous saying: 'If you do what you love, you will never work a day in your life.' This is exactly how it feels when you find your niche in the hospitality industry, so choose a job that you love to do.

Regardless of where you start – be it washing dishes, cleaning rooms, waiting on tables, working behind the bar or cooking in the kitchen – the beauty of the hospitality industry is that it is easy to progress and move around to gain the experience you want.

Hopefully these stories have inspired you to progress in your hospitality career. The next section will help you to do this by examining the soft skills that you will need to demonstrate – skills that will take you far in this industry.

SECTION 2

TOP TIPS FOR DEVELOPING YOUR CAREER IN HOSPITALITY

The word 'hospitality' means to be welcoming and friendly. The international symbol of hospitality is the pineapple. This dates back to the time of Christopher Columbus, when he was welcomed by villagers placing pineapples on their gate posts. In those days it was an exotic fruit and it was an honour to have a pineapple presented to you.

Being truly hospitable is an art. It comes down to basic etiquette and requires social interaction, which sadly is easier said than done these days. For some top tips on what to do when looking for a job in hospitality, I have used the word 'hospitality' as an aide memoire to help you remember some key points. (Please note that this section will not look at letter writing, putting together a CV or job applications, as there are many books and organisations that can help you to do these.)

I want to focus on the subtler, softer skills, which are not often talked about, but are exactly what an employer is looking for. Put these into practice today if you really want to impress.

Hello

Opportunities

Social media

Professionalism

Introductions

Talent

Attitude

LinkedIn

Initiative

Time Management

Yes I can

Let's look at why the way we say 'Hello' is so important.

Hello – it all starts with a 'Hello'

You will meet different types of people when you are looking for employment. How quickly you find employment will depend on many factors. One way to get ahead is to look at how you introduce yourself to a potential employer. If the first words that come out of your mouth are 'Give us a job, mate', you may have to knock on a few more doors before one opens for you.

I want you to imagine that you are going for a job interview and meeting the interviewer for the first time. When you meet them, more than likely the first word that you will say is 'Hello'. Knowing how to meet and greet someone in the correct manner is important if you want to work in hospitality. Now this may sound simple and straightforward, but how many times have you had someone come up to you and say 'Hiya! You alright?' or something similar? Immediately you will form an opinion of the person you have just met. The same will happen in an employment situation.

The words that you use set the standard of how you will socially interact with that person and the interactions that follow. It will demonstrate your attitude and lead to your behaviour. Let me give you an example of what I mean by this.

'Hiya' or 'You alright?' are informal ways to greet someone. This is normally an exchange used between friends who know each other well. This is quite possibly followed up with a hug or some other form of physical contact, such as a playful punch to the arm.

'Hello' is a general word used to greet people you may or may not be so familiar with. If saying this to someone you have met for the first time is followed up with a wave of the hand, it will indicate that you are trying to get someone's attention and are unsure of whom you are speaking to. However, extending your hand when saying 'Hello' will indicate a more confident way of introducing yourself as you prepare to shake the other person's hand.

'Good Morning' or 'Good Afternoon' are more formal ways of greeting people. This might be followed with a question or form of enquiry relayed in a confident manner.

All of the above are different ways of introduction, but the one you choose to use should be appropriate for your setting. Therefore, in a job interview situation, going down the more formal route initially would be your better option, although the way you say 'Hello' is just the start of your social interaction.

For some, meeting people for the first time can be quite awkward, particularly if you are shy. What can happen is that we greet the other person and then there is an uncomfortable silence. What are we meant to say next?

> ## Top tips on how to introduce yourself in a confident manner
>
> - Greet the other person and introduce yourself. By doing this they should give you their name too
>
> - Use their name at the earliest opportunity in the conversation: this shows that you have listened to them and are interested in them
>
> - Ask open questions to find out more about them or their organisation; they should give you more information from which you can build your conversation
>
> - Build rapport through the use of body language and mutual interests that may come up in the conversation; if you establish this connection with the other person, they will open up more to you, which will make the conversation flow more smoothly

Now this may seem straightforward, but it can go wrong quickly. To start with, we are not necessarily confident at going up to people and introducing ourselves; we tend to wait for the other person to make the first move. To show that you are confident and professional you have to be bold enough to approach people you don't know and start that conversation.

If the other person does not give you their name, there is nothing wrong in asking them for their name so you can then slip it into the conversation. When they have given their name to you, it is really important that you are actually listening to them so you remember it.

Listening is a skill that we are not always good at. Sometimes when we meet people we go into 'autopilot' mode:

Person A: 'Good Morning...'

Person B: 'I am fine thanks, how are you?'

Person A has not even finished introducing themselves or asked the question 'How are you?' Person B has taken it upon themselves to jump in and give a standard response. This is a clear example of someone not listening and just going through the motions. We only actually retain 25%–50% of what we hear, so listening is a key skill that needs to be practised.

When it comes to asking questions, we are also not necessarily good at asking open questions. Open questions will start with the words 'Who', 'What', 'Where', 'When', 'Why' and 'How'. By using any of these words to start a question the other person will respond with a more detailed answer. The problem is we tend to speak in closed questions and close our conversations down before we have even started. A closed question tends to elicit a 'yes' or 'no' answer.

I believe one of the reasons we do this is because as a child, your parents would have told you not to speak to strangers. If we listened to our parents, either we would have ignored strangers that may have approached us or shut down the conversation. In either case, this lack of interaction is very rude. Now, our parent's intention at the time was to protect us, but as we grow up we are then told to do the exact opposite.

Once we get the first three pointers right, it will be much easier to make that connection and build rapport with the other person so our conversation flows. The art of conversation is to come across as polite, professional and friendly.

Sometimes it is the 'friendliness' part that people can get wrong. These days, people are a lot more informal in the way they interact, but the boundaries of what is acceptable behaviour and what is too informal need to be understood. When working in hospitality your attitude and behaviour will take you far.

It is difficult to change someone's attitude, and you are the only person who can change your own behaviour. This is because you are the one who makes a choice of how to behave in a given situation. Everything else can be taught. Hospitality is a service industry, which means exactly that. You are there to serve your customers. This means you should be the type of person who can be told what to do and carry this out willingly. If you believe you have the right attitude, which is friendly, helpful, and customer focused; and you can behave in a polite and professional manner, you are on the right track to getting a job in hospitality.

It is also important to be consistent in the way you behave. Putting on a show for an interview is one thing. Being able to maintain that will only happen if it is the way that you naturally behave. Remember, anyone that you speak to is a potential employer, so next time you are talking to someone you don't know, think about how you come across. You never know where that conversation may lead.

Opportunities – the world is your oyster

As you can see from the various career stories in the first section of this book, the hospitality industry is vast. Whether you are starting your role as a kitchen porter, luggage porter, waiter, chef or bar person, the skills that you learn on the job are transferable. This literally means you can take them from one job to another.

This also means that in time you can move from one department to another or one sector to another, and even from one country to another. Hospitality is an international concern and if you want to travel the world and experience different cultures this is the industry to do just that.

A common mistake that a lot of people make is that they become comfortable with where they are at. They feel settled, but if you have ambition and you want to progress this will involve change and sometimes a little bit of risk. A 'job for life' is no more and these days people have 'portfolio careers' because they move around and gain different experiences. It may mean venturing into a new area, which is initially unfamiliar and perhaps a little scary. This is the challenge that will set you apart. Sometimes it is the small wins that we have that build into quantum leaps. If you want to progress your career, you always need to be looking out for your next opportunity.

To know which opportunities are right for you, you need to set some clear career goals. Consider the following question:

Where do you want to be in one year, three years and five years?

In the first section of this book I mentioned the famous saying 'If you do what you love, you will never work a day in your life', so think about what you enjoy and how you can combine that with your career. If you read Grant Ridley's career story, you will see that he has done exactly that. His passion for cooking led him to train as a chef.

Exercise

To help you set your career goals you need to write them in a SMART format:

Specific

Measurable

Achievable

Realistic

Timebound

Saying 'I want to be a chef', however, is much too vague. There are different chef roles and ways of training, from apprenticeships and college courses through to work experience.

As an example, to make the career goal smarter you would state:

'To become a commis chef in the next twelve months working in a fine dining restaurant, by obtaining a commis chef apprenticeship.'

In this way, to get your cheffing career off to a flying start, you won't be applying for just any chef role but specifically a commis chef apprenticeship role in a fine dining restaurant.

When you have set your own career goals, it will be easier for you to spot opportunities that will help you to achieve them. Remember, your career goals are not rigid, and they may evolve as you get more experience and become more focused.

Opportunities will present themselves, but you need to grab them or they may pass you by. I have had opportunities that have passed me by, and opportunities that I have taken. If I had walked into the Springboard offices when I was at school, my hospitality career may have taken a different route. If I had not taken the opportunity to meet with John Duffy when I was a passenger on the QE2 I may never have applied to work on the cruise ships and travelled the world.

There are many twists and turns in life, and you have to work out for yourself which path you want to take. There are different paths that could lead to the same destination but will give you very different experiences along the way. It is similar to when you are driving a car. To get from one place to another you might choose to take the slower B roads taking in the scenery, or you might want to fast track and use the motorway.

Keep your eyes open and look out for the opportunities that will present themselves. They will come in many different guises. It is not necessarily just job opportunities we are looking at here, but opportunities that present themselves while you are in the job.

It could be being nominated for an award. Keep yourself up to date with industry news. Find out about competitions and awards that you can enter. This might be an internal company award or a national award. Jack McCarthy was recognised for his outstanding guest service skills by being named Concierge of the Year at the Boutique Hotelier Awards. Alex Graeme is running an award-winning tour guiding company that has been given gold by Visit Devon on consecutive occasions. Neel Radia has won several Catey awards, one of the most prestigious industry awards, also referred to as the 'Oscar' of the hospitality industry (if you have not already, you can read their career stories in the first section of this book).

It might be getting involved in a specialist group, such as a focus group where your opinion counts, or joining a committee. Opportunities usually come about through conversations. You may have been speaking with someone and they recommend you for something. That is how I ended up becoming chair for the Institute of Hospitality London. It is important to expand your network and make as many contacts as you can and build on those relationships.

Don't wait to be asked though. Put yourself forward. The worst that could happen is that you are not selected or you are told 'no'. Don't let that defeat you. Sometimes it is about being in the right place at the right time. It could happen that opportunities may present themselves, but the timing might actually be wrong for you. That is why it is important that you are clear on where you want to be and know your goals. It is not just about getting a job; it is about working out where that job could lead you in your hospitality career.

Social media – there is no delete button

Social media is a fantastic way to find out about what companies are doing. As well as looking at a company's website to find out more about them, you should follow them on social media. This will give you an idea of what they believe in and a great insight into how much they value their employees. This is important, as you want to work for an employer that will look after you.

The Landmark London is a great example of this. They regularly post photos showcasing their employees and celebrating their successes. It is no surprise that they are in *The Sunday Times* Best 100 Companies to Work For, which is probably why Anna Napora has stayed with them for her entire career. You may remember her story featured in the first section of this book.

It is also a great way for companies to find out more about you and what you get up to. According to Smart Insights, the number of internet users worldwide in 2018 is 4.021 billion, up 7% year on year. The number of social media users worldwide in 2018 is 3.196 billion, up 13% year on year. Facebook has the most active daily users.

What goes on social media stays on social media. Now you might be thinking if I post something I can always delete it if I change my mind. On the internet there is no such button; you may think you have deleted it, but it is still out there in the ether.

In this time of selfies and camera phones, there is no escape and photos of you will end up on social media. Don't be quite so proud of those drunken antics that you have shared with your friends and posted, as they will come back to haunt you.

A white paper compiled by Walters reports on social media popularity and attitudes and reveals the percentage of job seekers who have a profile on the following accounts:

- LinkedIn: 85%

- Facebook: 74%

- Twitter: 39%

According to a survey carried out by CareerBuilder (2017), 70% of employers use social media to screen candidates before hiring them. Their findings reveal that employers use social media to look for the following:

- Information that supports candidates' qualifications for the job (61%)

- Whether the candidate has a professional online persona (50%)

- What other people are posting about the candidates (37%)

- For any reason at all not to hire a candidate (24%)

Have you ever googled yourself? That is what 69% of employers will do when using search engines to find out more about you. The sorts of things that will get your application turned down include:

- Candidate posting provocative or inappropriate photographs, videos or information (39% of employers would turn you down on these grounds)

- Candidate posting information about them drinking or using drugs (38%)

- Candidate making discriminatory comments related to race, gender or religion (32%)

- Candidate bad-mouthing their previous company or fellow employees (30%)

- Candidate lying about qualifications (27%)

Social media can be used to your advantage, as long as your profile is cleaned up and looks professional. Employers still want to see your character and that you have a healthy work–life balance – just keep your private moments private.

Professionalism – know your boundaries

When working in hospitality you will be in constant contact with people. You will be working in a busy environment, whether you work front-of-house, directly with customers, or back-of-house, working closely with your colleagues. At times, the stress levels will increase as you work towards tight timescales, and there will be a sense of urgency for you to complete your tasks.

Tips that will help you to maintain your professionalism
• Be smartly groomed and well presented – this presents a good image and will make you feel good about yourself
• Be early for meetings, appointments and trainings – this demonstrates good timekeeping
• Maintain a positive attitude – this shows your motivation
• Complete all tasks in a timely manner – this will show your organisational skills
• Support and work together with your colleagues – being able to work as a team is a key skill

By being professional at all times you will gain trust and respect from all of your customers. Customers are sometimes referred to as internal customers and external customers. Your colleagues are your internal customers, as you will be serving each other to get your job completed. As a waiter you cannot serve your customer their food unless your colleagues in the kitchen have the food ready in time. When working on reception, you cannot check a guest into a clean room unless housekeeping have that room ready for you and maintenance have repaired any defects. Your guests are often referred to as your external customers as they are paying for the service you are delivering.

Both your internal and external customers deserve the same level of professionalism. Sometimes mistakes will happen, and this is all part of the learning process. It might be down to a miscommunication or a misunderstanding. Whatever the reason, at some point you will end up in the firing line, so to speak. Whether this is coming from your manager, a colleague or a customer, the best way to deal with this is to stay professional at all times.

You need to remind yourself that the other person is angry or frustrated at the situation that has occurred and not necessarily angry at you personally. It just so happens that you are the person they are directing their anger towards. Take a deep breath and look for a solution to the challenge that has just presented itself to you. Thinking on your feet is something that you will learn to do as you get more experience in this fast-paced industry, although you need to have a calm head to be able to do this.

You may also be in a situation where you have made a mistake. If this happens, the best way to deal with it is to own up to it as soon as you realise it has happened and then you can get help to fix it. Don't think by ignoring it the issue will go away. If anything, the problem will just get worse. Highlighting it as early as possible will show your honesty and integrity. You will get more respect from your peers by handling it this way than by trying to hide it.

Knowing your boundaries is also vital when working in hospitality. Sometimes those boundaries can become a bit blurred, so you need to know what the limits are: what is acceptable and what is unacceptable.

Depending on your job role, it may involve chatting with your guests, drinking with your guests and dining with your guests. It does not mean sleeping with your guests.

Chatting with your guests – every employee will be encouraged to interact with their customers and this will mean striking up conversations with them. This is very important when we welcome our customers. This could involve talking about the weather, how their journey was and finding out a little more about them. What it does not involve is delving into their personal life; or getting their mobile number so you can ask them out on a date.

Drinking with your guests – in some job roles you may be required to have a drink with your guests. This might be a coffee or an alcoholic drink. The general rule is that you don't drink alcohol on duty… unless it is part of your job role. Entertaining guests may include having an alcoholic drink with them. This is absolutely fine, but you must know what your limits are. I am not just referring to the number of drinks that is acceptable to your organisation at such occasions, but also to know your own alcohol tolerance levels. If you end up drinking too much, it will affect your behaviour, which may lead to other undesirable outcomes. If in doubt, stick to water.

Eating with your guests – part of entertaining your guests may involve having a meal with them. Again, this may involve having alcohol. Remember, you are still representing your organisation when you do this and you are not on a date having a romantic dinner.

As long as you understand what the limits are with your organisation that you work for, and you know what is acceptable, you should be fine. Do remember, drinking alcohol on duty when not permitted and fraternising with your guests are behaviours that are not deemed acceptable and could result in a dismissal.

Introductions – be remembered for all the right reasons

Knowing how to introduce yourself is a key interpersonal skill and comes down to basic etiquette and communication. If you are going for a job interview, your potential employer would have met many candidates all wanting the same role as you. You need to ensure that you are remembered for all the right reasons and leave a lasting positive impression. Similarly, when working in hospitality, you want to leave a good impression with the guests and customers that you will be engaging with on a daily basis.

It is therefore important to have a basic understanding of the communication model, sometimes referred to as 7–38–55, which was created by Albert Mehrabian and is still widely used today. There are three parts to the communication model – verbal, vocal and non-verbal.

Verbal communication refers to the words that we use when we speak to each other. This represents 7% of the communication model. It is a very small percentage because, believe it or not, the words that we hear play a minimal part in how we receive a message when we communicate. What we do need to be aware of though is the choice of words that we use. Every industry has its own 'internal language', sometimes referred to as jargon or industry terms, and hospitality is no exception.

Let's look at some examples to demonstrate this. In hospitality, KP means 'kitchen porter', someone who washes the dishes in the kitchen. A person not working in our industry may associate it with a brand of peanuts. Likewise, a DM is a 'duty manager', or the manager who is on duty in the absence of the general manager of the establishment. Again, outside of our industry, this is a well-known type of boot manufactured by Dr Martens. The wrong choice of words can cause confusion and mixed messages.

The next part of the communication model is vocal, which represents 38% of the way we communicate. This refers to the way we speak: if we speak slowly, quickly, quietly or loudly, if we stress certain words in a sentence, and the general intonation we use. Your voice can be compared to a musical instrument. When you speak, your voice will go and up and down like a melodic flow. How we pitch the words in our sentence can also change the meaning.

A classic example of this can be seen in the following sentence:

'How are you *doing?*'

As this is a question, we will tend to start with a lower voice and then our voice will go a little higher as we stress the last word.

Now if you have ever watched the television sitcom *Friends* you will know that the character Joey has his own way of expressing this. He says 'How are *you* doing?' Stressing the word 'you' changes the meaning and turns the phrase into a much more flirtatious exchange of words.

The last part of the communication model is the most powerful as it represents 55% of the way we communicate, and that is through our non-verbal language. This means how we use our body language, from giving eye contact, nodding our head, the way we stand or sit, using gestures and even the way that we wear our clothes.

Imagine walking into a job interview and your shirt is untucked and creased – what impression have you just created? Or you are wearing a baseball cap backwards and do not take it off when you meet your interviewer?

Non-verbal communication is the first thing that we pick up on, because it is the first thing that we see or notice about something or someone.

You may have heard the expression 'a picture paints a thousand words'. Well, there is a lot of truth in that. When we look at an image and see something visually, we start to construct a story around what is happening. This is exactly what happens when we meet someone for the first time, or see something for the first time.

It is important to remember that the job interview is a two-way process. It is not just about whether your potential employer thinks you are the right person for the job, it is also about whether you think you will fit in with the organisation. Working in a high street pizza restaurant will be a different experience to working in a fine dining restaurant.

It is always a good idea to check out your potential place of work. If it is in a bar, restaurant or hotel, go there for a drink a few days before your interview and observe your surroundings. Watch the employees and see how they work together. Do they get along? Does the environment feel right for you? Do you think you would fit in? Always check out the toilets, as they will give you big clues as to what the back-of-house areas will be like. Are the toilets clean or are they neglected?

First impressions are made in the first three to five seconds of meeting someone. That impression is created initially by what is seen visually. This is why the way you are dressed is key.

Another tip before meeting your prospective employer is to go to the toilet and do a quick check of your appearance in the mirror. From the time you have left your home to the time you get to the job interview, all sorts of things can play havoc with the way you look. If it is a windy day, or it is raining, you may be looking a little wind swept, or your shoes may have become dirty. Likewise, if it is a beautifully sunny day, you may have become a little sweaty and might need to check your personal hygiene.

When you arrive at your interview, what you may not re-alise is that the staff members you interact with will also be assessing you. Think about it. You arrive at the building and you will have to tell someone, possibly a receptionist, that you have an appointment with the human resources manager, for example. The receptionist will contact human resources to let them know that you have arrived and will also tell them what their first impressions of you are. That is why the way you look and the way you introduce yourself at this point are key.

The way you meet and greet your interviewer is again very important. Remember what I said about the way you say 'Hello' (see 'H for Hospitality' at the start of this section).

Another thing you can do – something that your interviewer will not be expecting – is to have a business card ready to hand over. This would be a personal business card with your name and contact details, such as your email address and mobile number. You might also want to add your LinkedIn URL as a website. You could simply have your title as 'hospitality professional'. When you hand this over will depend on the situation; it might be more appropriate to hand this at the end of the interview, to leave a lasting impression.

Business cards can be made easily. There are several online companies that have templates you can use so you can design your own, and these can be printed and delivered to you for about £10. Also, bear in mind that the way you put together your business card will say something about you, so check for any spelling mistakes and make sure it represents you in a professional way.

Talent – focus on your strengths and remember there is always room for improvement

During your interview the interviewer will be assessing you on three things – knowledge, skills and attitude. These are the abilities and characteristics that you need to be able to demonstrate that you are the right person for the job. I like to think of these as your talents that you have to offer. First, let's look at your knowledge and skills, because attitude is a slightly different beast which has its own heading below.

To work in hospitality, you do not need to be knowledgeable or skilled at the start of your journey because these specific job-related skills can be taught. Many hospitality organisa-tions will be happy to train you and give you the knowledge and skills that you need to carry out your job. However, this does not mean you can sit back and you will automatically be given a job. What you need to be able to demonstrate in the interview is your understanding of the industry, the company you have applied to work for and your commitment and willingness to learn about the industry. As you progress up the career ladder, this is when your knowledge and skills will become more important.

The knowledge that you can demonstrate to your interviewer is that, at the very least, you have done your research on the company that you have applied to work for. This will mean looking at their website and finding out as much about them as you can. If you are applying for a position within a large organisation, do not fall into the trap of finding out just about the organisation as a whole. You must also find out about the particular site that you have applied to work at.

When I was human resource manager for Hilton Hotels and I was recruiting potential employees, I would ask my candidate what they knew about the hotel they had applied to work in. Nine times out of ten I would get the standard answer of Hilton has many hotels in London and worldwide. I would then repeat, what did they know about this particular hotel? Often, they would not be able to tell me.

To start with, they could easily have told me how many stars the hotel had and how many rooms, or the name of the restaurants, for example. All of this information is easily accessible on the hotel website or on sites such as TripAdvisor. Not knowing this information showed me that the candidates had not done their research and were not really interested in working in this particular hotel; they just wanted a job. It is knowing details like this that will set you apart from the other candidates.

You should also know about the position that you are applying for. Most organisations will send you a job description and person specification. A job description will give you an overview of the job and explain some of the tasks that you will be expected to carry out. A person specification will detail the type of person they are looking for.

These two documents hold vital clues as to what the interviewer will be assessing you on. They will highlight some of the knowledge and skills they require. As I mentioned earlier, if you are new to the industry you may not have specific knowledge and skills, but you will have transferable skills. It is important to demonstrate these. Transferable skills are life skills that you can use in any situation and will include:

- Communication skills

- Interpersonal skills

- Time management

- Team-working skills

- Planning and organising

- Problem solving... just to name a few

Think of real-life examples where you have used these skills so that you can explain them in the interview, as you will be asked about them. There are two ways in which you may have to demonstrate these in an interview.

If the interviewer wants to find out how you would deal with a customer complaint for example, they might give you a scenario and ask you how you would go about solving it. Or they might ask you to explain a specific time when you have had to deal with a customer complaint and what you did. Either way, you should be clear on how you can demonstrate these skills to your interviewer. This technique is called behavioural questioning. They are assessing how you will behave in a given situation.

Some job roles will also require more technical skills. For example, as a chef you need to have good knife skills. In such a case you may be offered a work trial, so your ability can be assessed. Any number of positions may offer a work trial, which is normally when you will work one shift alongside another member of staff. This might be in the kitchen, restaurant or bar, for example. This is your opportunity to show what you can do. It is also a great chance for you to find out more about the company you will be potentially working for and for your employer to see how you fit in with the team.

If a large organisation is recruiting for a number of job roles, they may invite you to attend an assessment day. This is a full day when many candidates will be assessed at the same time. You will be split up into groups, and throughout the day assessments will be carried out through a variety of techniques including interviews, presentations, group work and individual exercises. At these events, you will not only be assessed on how you complete the various tasks and how you come across in the interview, you will be assessed on how you interact with the other candidates and assessors.

Remember, whether you have been invited to attend an interview, trial shift or assessment day, you are constantly being assessed on your knowledge, skills and attitude by various people.

In these situations you need to show off your talents and play to your strengths. Really emphasise what you are good at and show your ambition. Two of the classic recruiter questions are:

- What are your strengths?

- What are your weaknesses? (or some may call them 'areas for improvement')

You need to acknowledge both of these and state them in a positive way. There is a fine line between boasting and showing confidence in your strengths. Never say you don't know what your weaknesses are, or that you do not have any. Nobody is perfect. Think about the skills that you would like to develop further.

Whatever answers you give, what is always showing is your attitude, so let's take a closer look at this.

Attitude – you are how you behave

The business dictionary defines attitude as: 'A predisposition or a tendency to respond positively or negatively towards a certain idea, object, person, or situation. Attitude influences an individual's choice of action, and responses to challenges, incentives, and rewards (together called stimuli).'

The reason your attitude is so important when working in hospitality is because it will be reflected in the way that you behave and interact with your customers and colleagues.

The way that our attitudes are set stems from our belief systems. Our beliefs are introduced to us at a young age, usually from our parents and schoolteachers. From these beliefs we develop our values, and these guide us to judge what is right and what is wrong, which then leads us to recognise what is acceptable and unacceptable behaviour. It is this constant repetition that 'programmes' us to respond to certain situations in a particular way.

To illustrate this, I am going to refer to Richard Bandler and John Grinder's NLP model of communication. NLP refers to neuro-linguistic programming, which looks at how we communicate and interact with others. We take information from outside and process it internally, reacting to it through our attitude and behaviour.

The image below gives an overview of how the NLP model of communication works:

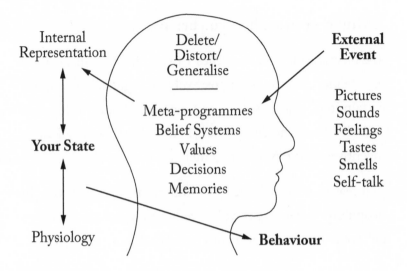

The NLP model of communication

Let's imagine an *external event* happens. You are faced with a customer who is crying. We will receive information from this external event through our senses – that is through what we see, hear, feel, taste, smell and even what we say to ourselves, referred to as self-talk.

We will then make an *internal representation* of that event in our heads. This will be different for different people, because it will be based on events that have happened to us in the past.

For example, the first time you encountered a customer crying, you may not have known how to deal with the situation at the time. Perhaps you did not deal with it well. How you handled that incident, that experience, will have been 'recorded' and you will remember it. Each time you are faced with a similar circumstance you will go back to that recording and react in the same way, as it is a learned behaviour. Sometimes that initial reaction may not have been the best way to deal with the situation. This means you have to unlearn or relearn a new behaviour.

To complicate things further, as we build our internal representation there are three components that will affect this. We will *delete, distort* and *generalise* the information we are receiving.

We delete information as we only pay attention to certain aspects of the experience. We need to do this as we cannot cope with the amount of information that we are receiving from all of our senses at that moment in time.

We will also distort the information we receive. So we change or misrepresent what is happening, or what we think we have just witnessed. Perhaps seeing this customer crying will make you think they are feeling sad when in fact it is not until you get closer that you realise they are crying tears of joy, not sadness.

The third thing that we do with the information we are receiving is *generalise* it. The conscious mind can only handle seven (plus or minus two) pieces of information at any given time. This means we oversimply things. So when we see someone crying, we will simplify the situation and might come to the conclusion that the person is upset. This will happen based on our past experiences of someone crying because they were upset.

It is through generalisation that we learn. From the information we are receiving we will put some meaning behind it and draw a conclusion from this. To come to those conclusions, the information we are receiving from the external event will also go through a set of five filters. These are *meta-programmes, belief systems, values, decisions* and *memories*. A meta-programme will essentially determine how we will react to a situation through our behaviour, feelings and emotions. There are several different meta-programmes. One example is proactive versus reactive:

- If we are proactive, we will act quickly and take the initiative

- If we are reactive, we will wait, consider and reflect

So in essence, when an external event happens, we take in the information from that event through our senses. As we process that information we will delete, distort and generalise it, and as it goes through our five NLP filters, we will then make an internal representation.

This internal representation will come about through our *state* and *physiology*. For example, how we are feeling emotionally at that moment in time, such as tired or calm. If we are tired, we may not deal with the situation very well; if we are feeling calm we will be in a better position to deal with our customer in a professional manner.

Our physiology can easily change our state of mind. This can be done simply by moving our body from a slouching position to standing up straight. When you are slouching you are relaxed, when you are standing upright you are more alert.

From this we will then react to the situation, which will show in the *behaviour* that we choose to display. We might ignore the customer, thinking they are okay and do not need our attention. This would be an example of the reactive meta-programme. Or we might approach them and share in their joyous moment, which is an example of the proactive meta-programme.

The key to this is that we choose how we want to behave in any given situation. It is those choices that we make at that moment in time that will show our attitude.

LinkedIn – it is never too early to build your network

As mentioned earlier in this section, 85% of job seekers have a profile on LinkedIn. It is common knowledge that employers do look at LinkedIn to find potential candidates and to do further research on job applicants. This means it is extremely important to have a presence on LinkedIn and that your presence shows you in a professional light.

Building your profile on LinkedIn: This is pretty straight-forward and involves filling in a set template online. What is crucial is the content that you put in the various sections.

First of all, you will be asked to enter your first and last name, hopefully no explanation needed for this. If you do have any post nominals, or letters after your name, then you can add these in the last name box after your surname, if you wish to.

You will then have a 'headline' to fill in. In this space you can write a short sentence about yourself. Most people use this to say what their current job role is – however you should use this to your advantage and write a short succinct sentence about who you are and what you are seeking.

For example, you might put 'Hospitality professional seeking role in a cocktail bar.' Doing this will increase your chances of potential employers and recruiters contacting you directly. Once you have secured a position, remember to update this to reflect what you are currently doing.

Continue to complete the template with the various job roles and education that you have, and include any volunteering experience you may have.

For your previous roles, ensure that your job title is clear to show what you did. For example, just putting 'team leader' is unclear but 'bar team leader' is more defined. Then write a short sentence or paragraph pulling out your key responsibilities and skills that you have used.

You will then have an opportunity to add your contact details. There are a couple of things you should do here:

Edit: Edit your LinkedIn URL or website address, which will direct people to your LinkedIn profile. This is automatically generated for you by LinkedIn and includes your name, although at the end there will be a series of numbers. You can simply edit this and take these numbers out so your LinkedIn URL is much neater and more succinct. For example my public LinkedIn URL is:

www.linkedin.com/in/monicaor/

Contact information: Remember I mentioned earlier about having your LinkedIn URL on your personal business cards? This is what you would use for your own profile. On the contact information section you can also add your telephone, address and email. Please remember this information will be available to the public. I would suggest only putting an email address here. With your email address, ensure it is suitable. Preferably set up an email with just your name and whichever email provider you use.

So for example, firstname.surname@gmail.co.uk. Having an account such as fluffybunny@gmail.co.uk really will not give the right impression.

Summary: You will then come to the summary section. This is one of the first sections people see when they view your profile. You should use this as an opportunity to introduce yourself. It will have more impact if you tell a short story about yourself and highlight your skills and experience.

To complete your summary section: An easy-to-use format is to complete the following statements:

I am...

I help others...

What I do is...

So that...

Which means that...

You don't need to use these exact words, but it will give you a framework of how to put together a short summary about yourself. To give you an example of how this works, imagine you are looking for work in a cocktail bar. You might say something like:

'I am an experienced mixologist. I introduce my customers to an exciting blend of alcoholic and fruit concoctions. I create these with theatre and engage my customers with my bar flairing skills. This keeps them entertained so they can have a relaxing and enjoyable experience in my bar.'

Photo: Now that you have completed the main content for your LinkedIn profile you need to add a photo of yourself. When it comes to your headshot there are a whole host of things you need to think of before uploading that photo. Photos that should never be uploaded to a LinkedIn profile include selfies, webcam photos, holiday snaps and snaps with other people in, particularly an ex-partner who you have tried to crop out. It is also just as important that you don't leave this blank and become an invisible person. If a headshot is not uploaded, the meaning behind this to a potential recruiter is that you are hiding something and so your profile will be overlooked immediately.

The headshot photo is all about you, and it should show you as a professional who is approachable. A simple head and shoulders image of just yourself with a blank background is all you need. You need to think about what you are wearing and what your body language is saying about you when you have this photograph taken. Remember, people will form a first impression in the first three to five seconds of seeing an image. The image they will be looking at on your LinkedIn profile is of you.

Now that you have your LinkedIn profile set up you are ready to connect with people in the industry. You can build your network gradually. Start by adding people that you know and then as time goes on you will start to get requests from people to be added to your network. Be selective in who you add to your network. It is not a competition to have as many contacts as possible.

Once you have built up your network you can ask people that you have worked with to post up a recommendation about you. They are basically giving you the equivalent of a reference that is visible on your profile, which will add to your credibility.

LinkedIn is a great platform to use to keep all your professional connections in one place. There will be times when you meet people and they give you their business card. There is always the old joke that you will then 'file' this away safely, in other words throw it in the bin, as you think you will never meet that person again, or you find it in your pocket a few months later and you cannot remember who they are.

There is a much better way to make use of that business card. Let's say you went to a careers fair and you collected several business cards. What you should do when you receive a business card – after the event, and certainly not in front of the person you have just met – is make a note on the card of where you met that person and something about them.

Then make a point of linking up with them on LinkedIn the next day and invite them to be a connection. It is important at this point not to fire off the standard email introduction that LinkedIn provide. You should personalise this and mention where you met. By introducing yourself in this way, the other person will remember you and will link up with you.

You now have access to more information on them and you can see their photo. In the future, if you arrange to meet again, you can take a quick look at their profile beforehand to remind yourself of what they look like. You can look at the messages you sent and this will remind you of where you first met. Then when you meet them the next time you can bring that up in conversation. Your new contact will be impressed that you remembered so much about them.

Sometimes you will connect with people on LinkedIn and you may think you will never meet that person again. The hospitality industry is very fluid and you never know when your paths will cross in the future.

Initiative – Be the difference that makes the difference

Hospitality is a fast-paced industry and you have to think on your feet. Your manager will not always be by your side guiding you step by step, they will expect you to take the initiative and make decisions at that moment in time. Your guest certainly won't have the patience to wait for you to get approval from your manager to take action. Your colleagues will need you to act quickly to ensure the smooth flow of service is not interrupted.

To do this you have to be alert and aware of what is going on in your surroundings. You need to be fully present. This does not mean just having a presence and physically being at your post. Standing there, looking pretty but being in a day dream, is of no use to anyone.

When you take the initiative you have to be able to read your guests' minds. You have to know your guests so well that you can anticipate their every need, before they even realise it was a need until you have fulfilled it for them. That is when your guests are going to think 'wow'.

In my second book *Star Quality Experience – The Hoteliers' Guide to Creating Memorable Guest Journeys* I refer to this as delivering 'random acts of kindness'. These are the small gestures that you make, without being asked, that have a great impact on your customer. Sometimes this is referred to as going the extra mile.

Delivering this level of service has to come from the heart. The key to this is that it is not a standard; it is a random act. So what you may do for one guest might be different to what you do for another guest. Remember all your guests have different needs and expectations.

A lot of organisations try to deliver this standard of service, but if the management and staff do not have a genuine understanding of what this entails, it can go horribly wrong. To give you an example of this, I once made a reservation for a birthday dinner at a restaurant and at the time of the booking I mentioned that it was for a birthday celebration. Immediately the lady who took my booking said, 'Oh, I will organise a birthday plate for you.' This means that when the dessert is plated, the chef will pipe on the side the words 'Happy Birthday'.

We had the meal in the restaurant and all was going well. When the time came for the waiter to take the dessert order, the person whose birthday it was decided that he did not want a dessert. I thought it would be interesting to see what the restaurant did next, as a birthday plate with no dessert really wouldn't be appropriate. For me, this would have been the perfect opportunity to deliver a random act of kindness. They knew it was a birthday celebration, so what could they have done to make it that extra bit special?

I was expecting them either to present a birthday plate with some sorbet and perhaps a candle in it – as my guest had said that he did not want a dessert, something light and refreshing like a sorbet would have worked – or maybe to offer a complimentary glass, or even better a bottle, of champagne, so the occasion could be toasted. No such luck. What they did was to present my birthday guest with an empty plate with the words 'Happy Birthday' piped on it. My guest was somewhat confused at this and really did not know what to do with the empty plate. I think he was then expecting to be presented with a birthday cake, but, alas, this did not happen either.

This is a classic example of how a supposed random act of kindness becomes a standard, one-size-fits-all response. The reason this does not work is because this is no longer a spontaneous gesture from the heart. Using your initiative is something that only you can do while you are fully present in the moment.

To find out more about delivering random acts of kindness you can see a whole gallery of examples that I have posted in the album called 'Random Acts of Kindness' on my Star Quality Hospitality Consultancy Facebook page, which can be accessed on this link:

www.facebook.com/StarQualityHospitalityConsultancy/

By using your initiative you will make a big difference to the experience of your guests and colleagues. Think about how you can do things differently.

Time management – if you are on time, you are late

Time management is an essential skill when working in hospitality. Most hospitality establishments are open 24 hours a day, 7 days a week. This means to run effectively, the team will be working shifts. The different shift patterns will depend on the department that you work in.

Typical eight-hour shifts might include:

Early shift – 7am to 3pm

Middle shift – 9am to 5pm

Late shift – 3pm to 11pm

Night shift – 11pm to 7am

During a week you could work any mixture of these shifts. Some of these shifts may end up being back to back, so for example, one day you might be on a late shift and the next day you could be on an early shift.

In some departments it is not uncommon to do twelve-hour shifts, such as 8am to 8pm. With this shift pattern you would normally work four days on and then have four days off.

Some establishments will operate split shifts, so you work a few hours in the morning, have a few hours off during the day and then return to work a few more hours in the evening to make up an eight-hour shift.

Regardless of the shift pattern the organisation that you work for uses, it is imperative that you are at work in good time. Due to the nature of shift work, your colleagues cannot go home until you arrive and take over from them. This inevitably will also include some form of handover.

In the hospitality industry we often say if you are on time you are late. This is because if your shift starts at 3pm, you are expected to be in your department at 3pm, not walking into the building at 3pm. You then have to allow time to get changed into your uniform and get to your post. In some establishments this could easily take another fifteen minutes.

Tardiness is not tolerated in the hospitality industry because this will ultimately result in keeping your customer waiting. Remember, your internal customers – your work colleagues – are just as important as your paying guest.

When we talk about time management we are not just looking at arriving at work in good time. We also need to take into consideration completing tasks on time. I will always remember when I was training to be a chef and we were making custard in the college kitchen, which was to be served to paying guests in our college restaurant.

I stood there patiently stirring my custard, which was taking longer than expected to thicken up. I had my chef lecturer asking where the custard was, and I was still standing there stirring it. 'It's not ready chef', I said. 'Not good enough, you can't keep the customer waiting,' was his response. Of course he was absolutely right. I was in a training situation so it was not the end of the world, but it did make me think about the sense of urgency that is needed when working in hospitality.

To help organise your day you need to plan ahead. This may mean taking half an hour to work out what needs to be done in order of priority.

When I was speaking to Mitch Collier from Le Manoir, he told me that chef founder Raymond Blanc asks his team at the hotel to focus on five things that they want to complete that day and ensure they are completed. This is a great work ethic, and it is a lot easier said than done. Five things does not sound very much but you will be surprised at how you get distracted or other issues come up that also need your attention. In hospitality inevitably this will involve your other team members and your guests.

It is important to stay focused on the task in hand. You do also need to factor in that there will be interruptions, as that it is the nature of our business. You also need to have a back-up plan, as things do go wrong, and allow more time than you think you need for the tasks you have to complete.

Setting yourself deadlines is a good way to work out what needs to be done and when. Set these throughout the day to keep yourself on track. You could also set reminders for yourself.

You are not Superman or Wonder Woman and you need to acknowledge you cannot do everything. Learn to prioritise your work – some of the less urgent things can wait and do not need an immediate response. You need to learn to work proactively rather than reactively, otherwise you will end up firefighting, which is no good for anyone.

You also need to remember there is a reason that you work in a team, so responsibilities can be shared out. When you get to supervisory or managerial level you need to learn how to delegate, which is a skill that people find difficult to do.

A lot of time is wasted in endless meetings. You should set a clear agenda prior to the meeting and have a finishing time for the meeting. There is a reason why team briefings are called briefings. They should last no more than ten minutes and team meetings should be no longer than an hour. You need to stick to the point and not go off on a tangent.

I remember once, when I was running a meeting for my heads of departments, I played the song 'A Little Less Conversation' (a remix of an Elvis Presley song with JXL) to get this point across. The lyrics of the songs are 'a little less conversation, a little more action, please.' That certainly got their attention. If you want to hear the song, you can watch the video on YouTube – search for Junkie XL, Elvis Presley – A Little Less Conversation (Elvis vs JXL).

Essentially, you need to be managing your own time. Avoid becoming a busy fool, working longer and harder than you need to. Use the advice above to work smarter.

Yes I can – always be the first to offer assistance

The hospitality industry is a service industry first and foremost, which means you have to be the type of person who is happy to go above and beyond the call of duty, take action and get things done.

I think this is also one of the reasons why people get so much satisfaction from working in this industry, because every day you get results no matter where you are working.

As a housekeeping assistant cleaning rooms, you go into a room which is usually a tip. Let's face it, your average hotel guest is not going to tidy up after themselves, that is one of the reasons for booking into a hotel in the first place. After twenty to thirty minutes you will have made that room pristine once more.

As a chef you have your *mise-en-place* or set-up of raw ingredients from which you produce a tantalisingly delicious meal. You know your guest is going to savour it and share photos of it all over social media. There's nothing like a bit of food porn.

It is a bit like watching those television make-over programmes with the 'before' image, where the room is looking drab and dated, and then after a spruce up, it is transformed into a thing of beauty. Imagine experiencing that feeling of satisfaction and achievement every day when at work. It all comes down to having that little bit of creativity and producing something that will be appreciated by the next person who experiences it.

It is not just about carrying out your own tasks; it is also about being there for others, namely your work colleagues and your guests. Taking on additional responsibilities should not be a chore, but a pleasure. If you are the type of person who can do this, it shows that not only do you take pride in your work, you know how to pay great attention to detail, and you show how much you care through the way that you carry out your duties.

The concierge department is fantastic at doing this. Whatever their guest requires, nothing is impossible. In a recent interview for Business Insider UK, members of Les Clefs d'Or revealed some of the more bizarre requests that they received, which included planning a $15,000 wedding for two dogs, and another guest wanting to have a meeting with the Archbishop of Canterbury arranged. The motto of the concierge team at The Pierre in New York is: 'The impossible will be done immediately and the extraordinary will take a few moments longer.'

It really does not matter where you work in hospitality, the true art to being hospitable is to always be the first to offer assistance and have a 'Yes I can' attitude. This is what will get you noticed. This is what will give you variety in your work. This is what will open up the doors of opportunity for you.

In this second section of the book we have looked at how you can develop your 'H.O.S.P.I.T.A.L.I.T.Y.' skills. It is down to you to act on this and put these tips into practice. A quick reminder of the aide memoire:

Hello	It all starts with 'Hello'
Opportunities	The world is your oyster
Social media	There is no delete button
Professionalism	Know your boundaries
Introductions	Be remembered for all the right reasons
Talent	Focus on your strengths and remember there is always room for improvement
Attitude	You are how you behave
LinkedIn	It is never too early to build your network
Initiative	Be the difference that makes the difference
Time management	If you are on time you are late
Yes I can	Always be the first to offer assistance

SECTION 3 –

OPENING DOORS: WHERE TO GET FURTHER ADVICE, GUIDANCE AND TRAINING

In the first section of this book you would have read the inspiring career stories of professionals currently working in the hospitality industry. The second section of this book has shown you what you need to do to be ready for a career in hospitality. This last section will introduce you to some of the organisations that can help you on your hospitality journey, irrespective of the stage you are at in your career and your background.

You may be starting out from school, working in a different industry and looking for a change, unemployed, or fallen on hard times. Whatever your circumstance, there is an organisation that can assist you in getting a rewarding career in this vibrant industry.

Charities to help kick-start your hospitality career

I am going to introduce you to three organisations that can help to get you started in hospitality. These are: the Springboard Charity, Beyond Food Foundation and The Clink Charity.

Springboard and The Clink are both charities, and Beyond Food Foundation is a social enterprise. The main goal of these organisations is to complete a social mission and to make a positive difference to the world of hospitality.

Both charities and social enterprises reinvest their profits into things that benefit a part of society, or society as a whole. For both types of organisation, sustainability is paramount. In order to continue to do good, the business must operate efficiently and effectively.

While charities tend to fund their good work through donations and fundraising, social enterprises often sell products or services to reinvest their profits.

Anne Pierce, the chief executive of Springboard, explains that there are two arms to the organisation: the Springboard Charity and Springboard UK, which works with employer partners to promote the hospitality industry.

Springboard

The Springboard charity has several initiatives to help people find employment in the hospitality industry and provides career advice, entry level training and work experience opportunities. Below is an overview of some of their initiatives:

'FutureChef' started off as a four-stage competition and has evolved into a year-long programme to encourage school children aged twelve to sixteen to develop their cookery skills. This inspires them to train as a chef and become the next James Martin.

Their 'Kickstart' programme is open to both school and college leavers who are sixteen or older. It is a three-week programme that helps them transition from education to employment, where they can experience work tasters, short course qualifications and two weeks' work experience with an industry employer.

Their 'IntoWork' programmes help people through training, placement, employment and mentoring to support them back into the workplace. One such programme is 'Galvin's Chance', which was initiated by chef patron Chris Galvin and general manager Fred Sirieix of the Galvin at Windows restaurant. It specifically helps those aged between eighteen and twenty-four who are not in education or employment and are at risk of knife and gun crime, offering them an alternative. They are given on-site training to gain a Level 2 qualification in front-of-house food and beverage service. This leads to opportunities to work in some of the most prestigious hotels, restaurants and food service operations.

> **Advice from Anne Pierce**: 'Explore all of the options because there is such a big choice out there. Quite often the job that is going to suit you the most is not always that obvious. It might be hidden behind the scenes, or it might be working with an organisation that is associated with the industry. There is such a variety of opportunities within this industry; it is really worth exploring to find the right slot for you.'

For more information on the Springboard Charity and how they can help you with your hospitality career, watch the full video with Anne Pierce here:

www.vimeo.com/265209163

Beyond Food

The Beyond Food Foundation was set up by Simon Boyle and offers a series of training programmes to assist vulnerable adults and homeless people to get a career in hospitality. It is based at the Brigade restaurant, which is also run by Simon.

The courses start off with a general focus on wellbeing and move on to employability skills. After this, attendees can join an apprenticeship, either front-of-house in the restaurant and bar, or in the kitchen, gaining work experience initially at the Brigade. Simon then helps them to find other work experience in the hospitality industry.

Chefs who join the apprenticeship will be given two years' solid work experience as they train – one year at The Brigade and another year at another hospitality establishment – and will qualify with a professional chef's diploma, which will set them up for a promising career.

Grant Ridley was one of Simon's apprentices and he is now working as a fine dining chef. You may remember his career story in the first section of this book.

> **Advice from Simon Boyle**: 'You have really got to want to do it because it takes everything you have got. If you really want to do it, it is easy and it is really enjoyable. You have got to be happy and engaged every day, and you have got to be willing to give everything and work hard.'

For more information on Beyond Food Foundation and how they can help you with your hospitality career, watch the full video with Simon Boyle here:

www.vimeo.com/266690026

The Clink

The Clink provides training for prisoners and helps with rehabilitation back into the workplace. Their sole aim is to reduce reoffending. The Clink operates training restaurants in prisons, where prisoners can gain qualifications in food service and practical experience in a fine dining environment.

Currently, Clink restaurants operate within prisons in Brixton, in London; High Down, in Surrey; Cardiff, in Wales; and Styal, in Cheshire.

The Clink has a five-step programme in which prisoners are recruited in the last six to eighteen months of their sentence. They are supported through their training, which leads to a City and Guilds qualification, and twelve weeks before their release they are introduced to a support worker who makes sure they have somewhere to live, a CV, a disclosure letter and a bank account. They are met at the gate and taken to their accommodation, taken to employment and reintroduced back into society. They are given support twenty-four hours a day, seven days a week.

Chris Moore, the chief executive, says, 'Nationally, 47% of people who leave prison go back to prison within the first year. With The Clink programme looking after people both sides of the wall we have now got this down to a sub-10% rate'.

> **Advice from Chris Moore**: 'The hospitality industry is great fun. It is a way of life and it is certainly something you can do well at, even if you have not done particularly well at school. To actually work as part of a team, as a family and to take responsibility – it is a great industry to be in.'

Watch the full video with Chris Moore to find out more about The Clink:

www.vimeo.com/266753423

The apprenticeship route and education

Apprenticeships date back to the Middle Ages, but these days the way apprenticeships work has changed. Apprentices are aged 16 or over, in employment and studying for a work-based qualification.

There are currently six new hospitality apprenticeship standards, which came into effect from May 2017:

Level 2 – commis chef/hospitality team member

Level 3 – chef de partie/production chef/hospitality supervisor

Level 4 – hospitality manager

With the new apprenticeships there must be a genuine need for training for at least twelve months in a new job role. This means that an existing employee can carry out an apprenticeship as long as their role is new and they need training in it.

There is no mandatory qualification and the training is flexible, which means the employer can choose the methods in which they train their staff. Some of the training (20%) must be off job, so an example of this could be online learning.

The employer needs to be confident that their apprentice is competent. After the twelve months' apprenticeship, an independent assessor will carry out an end-point assessment in which the apprentice is graded with a pass or distinction.

All apprenticeship training providers have to be government approved. You can search for an apprenticeship on this link:

www.gov.uk/apply-apprenticeship

Umbrella Training and Employment Solutions, a hospitality apprenticeship provider, works with business partners who

are industry employers in the five-star hotel market to provide apprenticeships on different pathways – from Level 2
through to degree apprenticeships.

The two main pathways are the hospitality pathway and the
chef pathway. The hospitality pathway starts with hospitality
team member, which is Level 2; this moves up to hospitality
supervisor, which is Level 3, and hospitality manager at
Level 4.

Within the hospitality team member apprenticeship, there
are also specialisms to choose from:

- Food and beverage service

- Alcoholic beverage service

- Barista

- Food production

- Concierge and guest services

- Housekeeping

- Reception

- Reservations

- Conference and events organisation

Within the hospitality supervisor apprenticeship, the specialist areas are:

- Food and beverage supervisor

- Bar supervisor

- Housekeeping supervisor

- Concierge supervisor

- Front office supervisor

- Events supervisor

- Hospitality outlet supervisor

Similarly with the hospitality manager apprenticeship, the specialist areas are:

- Food and beverage service management

- Housekeeping management

- Front office management

- Revenue management

- Conference and events management

- Hospitality outlet management

- Kitchen management (head chef)

- Multi-functional management

The chef pathway has the commis chef at Level 2; chef de partie at Level 3; and production chef at Level 3.

Umbrella Training is also working in partnership with the University of Kent and the University of Surrey to provide apprenticeship degrees.

> **Advice from Adele Oxberry, managing director at Umbrella Training**: 'This is a brilliant and friendly sector that will offer you opportunities and promotions, especially if you have the right attitude. You must like people and carry a smile every day, even in difficult situations. #GetHiredForYourSmile.'

For more information on how to get an apprenticeship with an employer, watch the full video with Adele Oxberry here:

www.vimeo.com/267770119

If you have very little industry experience and you are coming straight from school, the more traditional route into the hospitality industry is through education at college. You may study for a more generic degree qualification after your GCSEs and A-Levels, such as business studies, or a more specialist degree in hospitality management or culinary arts, for example.

The content of these degree programmes change and adapt with the times. As well as the usual core subjects such as business, marketing, finance and human resources, you will have more specialist subjects to choose from, such as e-business and web design, gastronomy, rooms division, events, small business and entrepreneurship, practical cookery or culinary science.

Another option is to get a degree while in full-time employment. These days, many people will combine their work and study for a foundation degree initially, and then top this up to a full honours degree on a part-time basis thereafter.

Work experience is extremely important and many college courses will include work experience elements within their curriculum, regardless of the level that you are studying at. College courses are not just aimed at school leavers; whatever level of education you have, there is a course that will suit your needs and pathways that will get you to where you want to be.

Westminster Kingsway College is the home of the award-winning School of Hospitality and Culinary Arts. The college was established more than 100 years ago when a committee of academics and hospitality representatives, including Auguste Escoffier and Isidore Salmon, came together to develop a school for professional cookery.

The first course to be developed has evolved into the Professional Chef Diploma, also known as the Westminster Diploma, and is still going strong today. It is the oldest culinary diploma in the UK.

Gary Hunter, the college's vice-principal, explains in his interview that the college runs hospitality and culinary arts courses from Level 1 through to degree level. The college is known for its strong industry connections and work experience opportunities that it offers to its students as part of their courses. As a specialist hospitality school, the college also offers bespoke courses along with mainstream qualifications.

Alumni of Westminster Kingsway College include popular TV chefs Jamie Oliver, Ainsley Harriott and Anthony Worrall Thompson.

Advice from Gary Hunter: 'You must select the right path for you. It could be an apprenticeship or a full-time course. It is about trying to be the best: it is about tasting the elements of everything we have to offer in the hospitality industry; about being able to experience as much as possible and selecting the right training institution that will give you a vast selection of really high quality experiences.'

Watch the full video with Gary Hunter for more information on the training, qualifications and industry experience that Westminster Kingsway College can provide:

www.vimeo.com/266773579

If you are looking to study for a degree and also get work experience in a commercial hotel at the same time, you might consider studying at The Edge Hotel School. This is the only hotel school in the UK. Students are given practical experience as they work at Wivenhoe House Hotel, which is a four-star commercially-run hotel in Essex.

Studying and working on rotation, the students will spend several weeks in the classroom, and then several weeks working in the hotel, and rotate throughout their two-year degree. This is an accelerated programme. At the first level they will work as an operative, at the second level they will work as a supervisor and in their final year they will work as a duty manager in the hotel.

The students will work in various departments in the hotel alongside their studies, including the kitchen, restaurant, conference and banqueting, housekeeping, reception and reservations. This is one of the few degrees in the country where the students can learn about and get hands-on experience in housekeeping, which is one of the key departments in any hotel.

Andrew Boer, the principal, says, 'Often you will get students who are quite shell shocked in their first few weeks because they will be asked to put on the Marigold gloves and go and sort out a toilet. Well, that's what all hotel managers have to do.'

Students will graduate with a BA (Hons) degree in hospitality management or a BA (Hons) events management with hospitality. The Edge Hotel School prides itself on the industry links it has. Students are involved and engaged with industry employers throughout their studies and encouraged to actively network with the industry. By the time they graduate, 94% of their students will have gained employment. Within one year of graduating, one student became head housekeeper at a London hotel and within two years of graduating another student became general manager of a Premier Inn.

Advice from Andrew Boer: 'You have got to be passionate about hotels, restaurants, clubs, bars and events, otherwise this is not the right place for you. It is about passion for the industry, it is about love of what you do and it is about interacting with people. Make this the central part of your life, because you are going to be spending a lot of your time doing this.'

More information about The Edge Hotel School and the full video with Andrew Boer can be found here:

www.vimeo.com/273102223

Having an industry mentor – bringing education and employers together

The secret to a lot of people's success is their ability to have a mentor as they progress throughout their career.

Peter Ducker, chief executive of the Institute of Hospitality, says, 'Mentoring is one of the greatest gifts that one can receive at any stage of their career.'

Mentoring is when two people – the mentee and the mentor – meet regularly and share experiences to help the mentee progress in their career.

The mentor will be someone who has knowledge and experience in the industry and can guide the mentee to make the choices that are appropriate for them through the use of questioning and listening. The mentor does not tell their mentee what to do, but will open them up to ideas to consider so the mentee can work out the best path for them.

Mitchell Collier from Le Manoir aux Quat'Saisons says, 'Hospitality is not only a delivery of service, it is an education system. There is this huge wealth of knowledge that professionals have and it is about sharing that with the next generation that is coming up after us.'

Whatever stage you are at in your career, there is always the option to have a mentor. The Springboard charity runs a mentoring programme called Springboard Gems, which is aimed at university undergraduates in their second year or above in hospitality-related courses. They will put students in touch with experienced industry managers for one-to-one mentoring and professional skills development. This initiative also enables colleges and universities to develop stronger industry links.

Westminster Kingsway College also has a strong focus on mentoring for their students, as do most colleges and universities.

Gary Hunter from Westminster Kingsway College says, 'For adults looking for a career change, we can help you with your career path and mentor you through your career change. What you should be looking for is a partner that works alongside your career.'

The Institute of Hospitality also offers a mentoring programme called 'Mentor Me' for their members, where student affiliates and associates can be mentored by a member or a fellow of the Institute (a fuller explanation of affiliates, associates, members and fellows can be found in 'Becoming an industry professional', further in this section).

Peter Ducker from the Institute of Hospitality says, 'Mentoring is enormously important, especially in an industry like ours, which benefits so much from the empathetic skills of its people.'

These days, a lot of industry professionals will only be too happy to mentor you. For the more established hospitality professional it is their way of giving back to the industry. This is another reason why networking and building your relationships with industry contacts is so important. Remember, in the second section of this book the 'L' in hospitality is all about using LinkedIn to build your network.

To find out more about the mentoring process, watch the video with Peter Ducker as he explains the importance of having an industry mentor:

www.vimeo.com/273869869

Another way you can find a mentor is through entering competitions where mentoring is part of the prize. You can read more about these opportunities next.

Winning awards – The Gold Service Scholarship, the Acorn Awards and the Cateys

There are numerous industry awards that recognise the skills and talents of those working in our industry, some of which have already been mentioned in the first section by our hospitality professionals that have shared their inspiring career stories. In addition to these, I would like to mention three very prestigious awards, namely the Gold Service Scholarship, the Acorn Awards and the Cateys. All three of these awards celebrate the success of people, from those starting out in their careers to those establishing their careers.

The Gold Service Scholarship, whose patron is Her Majesty The Queen, is aimed at people aged between 20 and 28, working full time in a front-of-house food and beverage position. The initial application is made online and there are four rounds, which assess both technical and social skills. The award is worth its weight in gold in terms of the educational opportunities it brings to the winning scholar. Past winners have even had their award presented by the Queen herself.

Edward Griffiths, a trustee and chairman of the judges for this scholarship, says: 'The idea of the scholarship is to encourage more young people into the industry and very specifically to put an emphasis on excellence and service.'

The winners receive both educational and mentoring opportunities: all the finalists go on a trip to Champagne to learn about the making of wine and champagne, and the winning scholar can choose from a number of different prizes, which may include working at Buckingham Palace for a state visit, or a week's work experience placement at the Mandarin Oriental Hotel, The Waterside Inn or Le Gavroche.

Michael Staub, who works as the floor manager at the Holborn Dining Room at The Rosewood London, was the 2018 Gold Service Scholar. He had only been working in the industry for two years when he entered the competition.

Michael talks about his experience: 'During the competition, over a course of six months, you get the chance to meet the future leaders of the hospitality industry; you get to connect with people who share your passion... the trustees and all the judges of the competition are so motivated and so passionate about sharing their advice to help you grow in the industry... With the placements, I got some unique opportunities to learn and grow and to acquire new skills, which would have been impossible to achieve without the Gold Service Scholarship.'

Advice from Michael Staub on entering the Gold Service Scholarship: 'Just go there, do what you know, have a big smile and share your passion for this industry.'

Advice from Edward Griffiths: 'This is a great industry and it has wonderful opportunities for young people, and there are wonderful careers available.'

For more information on the Gold Service Scholarship, watch the full video with Edward Griffiths and Michael Staub, the 2018 Gold Service Scholarship winner:

www.vimeo.com/268596523

The Acorn Awards, which are affectionately known as the '30 for under 30s' awards, have been around since 1986, and are awarded through *The Caterer* magazine. There are just 30 winners, all aged under 30, chosen from all areas of hospitality. The awards recognise the rising stars in the industry who clearly demonstrate their flair and passion.

To enter there are only three criteria:

- You must be in the hospitality industry

- You must be under the age of thirty by a specific date (usually at the start of June)

- You must be able to attend the winner's weekend held in June

Nominations are usually closed at the end of January for the winners to be chosen to attend a weekend away in June to celebrate their achievements.

In 2018 Jack McCarthy, who was featured in the first section of this book, was awarded an Acorn Award and took part in the celebratory weekend that was held at The Lygon Arms.

The Catey awards are known as the 'Hospitality Oscars' and have been running since 1984. Recipients are nominated, selected and judged by the industry through *The Caterer* magazine. The Hotel Cateys were launched in 2007 and the Food Service Cateys in 2013.

You may remember from our inspiring career stories that Sebastian Dabrowski was nominated for the Hotel Catey Executive Housekeeper of the Year Award in 2016 and Neel Radia won the Extra Mile Food Service Catey in 2015 for his volunteering work and was also named Public Sector Caterer of the Year in 2017 and 2018.

As mentioned earlier, the above are just three of the competitions and awards that are held each year for the hospitality industry – you can be nominated for many other industry awards. The hospitality industry is great at rewarding the talent within it. Gaining an industry award is not only a wonderful accolade to have; it opens doors to even more opportunities for you.

Becoming an industry professional

To get further advice and assistance throughout your hospitality career there are several professional bodies and industry associations that you can join. In this section I will mention just a few of them and share with you how membership of these organisations can be of benefit to you.

The Institute of Hospitality

The Institute of Hospitality is one of the main international professional bodies for the hospitality industry. It was formed in 1971 and was originally called the Hotel Catering Institutional Management Association (HCIMA) came about from the joining of two previous bodies – the Hotel and Catering Institute, which was established in 1949, and the Institutional Management Association, which was established in 1938. In 2007 the HCIMA was renamed the Institute of Hospitality (IOH).

The Institute of Hospitality is the professional body for managers and aspiring managers in the hospitality, leisure, travel and tourism industries and has a presence throughout the UK and globally.

Its vision is 'to provide international hospitality professionals with the highest professional standards of management and education in the hospitality, leisure and tourism sectors and help them become the best and most sought after managers within the industry.'

Its mission is 'to support and help our members achieve their highest potential within the industry through professional recognition, membership status, education and continued professional and personal development.'

Peter Ducker, chief executive of the Institute of Hospitality, explains: 'Our mantra is to promote professionalism through lifelong learning, which means from the day people start studying or entering the industry right through to when they retire.'

The Institute of Hospitality supports its members in a variety of ways. It has an extensive library, it commissions research on the latest trends, and publishes working papers, reports and management guides. It holds networking events, runs webinars and masterclasses, and has a mentoring programme for members to mentor other members.

There are several different membership grades, from which designated letters can be used after your name to demonstrate your achievement:

Affiliate membership is available to everyone working in the industry at any level and is automatically given when you first join the Institute of Hospitality.

Based on your industry experience and education you can then upgrade your membership to the following:

Associate (AIH) is usually for those working as a team leader, first line manager, supervisor or junior manager. The designatory letters AIH can be used after your name.

Member (MIH) is for senior managers, middle managers or heads of department. The designatory letters MIH can be used after your name.

Fellow (FIH) is usually awarded to managing directors, owners, CEOs or general managers who have demonstrated their commitment to the industry. The designatory letters FIH can be used after your name.

Advice from Peter Ducker: 'Go for it. It is the most wonderful career. It takes you anywhere in the world that you want to go and it is a true meritocratic industry where cream rises, where, if you have talent, if you have passion for the industry, you can achieve whatever level you set your sights on. Take advice, find a mentor, be guided, be helped and always remember that you are in charge of your own career.'

More information on the Institute of Hospitality and the full video with Peter Ducker can be found here:

www.vimeo.com/273845497

Other professional associations

There are also other associations that focus on membership for people working in a specific discipline. In the first section of the book, Mark Godfrey spoke about the **Master Innholders**, an organisation for established hotel managers. The award of Master Innholder is given to practicing hoteliers with a minimum of five years' experience as a general manager. They must have clearly demonstrated not only their hotel management ability but their continuing support for improving standards within the industry.

For chefs, the **Craft Guild of Chefs** has developed into the leading chefs' association in the UK and has many members globally.

You would have heard Jack McCarthy speak about **Les Clefs d'Or**. The Golden Keys Society is a professional association of hotel concierges. Easily identifiable by the golden crossed keys on their lapels, these members are an élite fraternity, globally connected, committed to professional development, and driven to setting new standards in guest service perfection.

Hotel receptionists can become members of the **AICR** which is an international association that stands for **the Amicale Internationale des Sous Directeurs et Chefs de Réception des Grand Hôtels,** or the **International Association for Deputy Managers and Front Office Managers of Luxury Hotels.**

There is the **Food and Beverage Managers Association** in London, which is accessible for food and beverage managers or directors of four- and five-star hotels or clubs and contract catering in Greater London. The association aims to promote the highest professional standards of management, education and recruitment in the food and beverage hospitality industry and to share best practice among its members.

For those in the licensed trade there is the **British Institute of Innkeeping**, which is the professional body that works across the industry to promote professional standards, well-managed, profitable businesses and responsible drinking. The institute provides advice and support to its members.

For barmen there is the **United Kingdom Bar Tenders' Guild**, which runs training and competitions at international level.

The UKHA is the **United Kingdom Housekeepers Association**, which was set up over thirty years ago. It is a support network for housekeepers, run by housekeepers throughout the UK. The organisation also works hard to promote housekeeping as a great career to have within hospitality.

Housekeeping is very often a career that is overlooked by many, as people think it is just a cleaning job, although, as has been seen in the interviews in the first section of this book, most people start in a cleaning role and rapidly progress in their careers.

Lorraine Dale is the national chair and the London chair for the UKHA and she explains: 'It allows housekeepers on the first steps of their career path to network and meet other housekeepers. If they have a problem they can talk to other housekeepers.'

One of the key events the Housekeepers Association holds is an annual Shared Knowledge Day, where key speakers give presentations and run workshops alongside a tradeshow. This sharing of knowledge keeps the housekeepers updated with the trends and changes in the industry, along with social events throughout the year.

Advice from Lorraine Dale: 'Come and try housekeeping as a career choice. It is a great way to start on the ladder into the industry. It is also a career where you can progress quickly and it covers many different angles, from dealing with budgets, dealing with day to day issues and solving problems. You also have stock control, you do refurbishments, you set standards and you meet people, so it is a really varied career. If you want to be a general manager, housekeeping is a good base.'

To find out more about the UK Housekeepers Association, the full video with Lorraine Dale can be found here:

www.vimeo.com/273119767

One final organisation that is important to know about is the IHSM, which is the **Institute of Hotel Security Management**. The safety and security of hotel guests and staff is paramount, particularly in this political climate. The IHSM is the UK's membership organisation for hotel security professionals who work closely with various law enforcement agencies. Their sharing and exchange of information helps to prevent, detect and deter crime in the hospitality industry.

These are some of the main professional bodies and associations that you can join. While this list is by no means exhaustive, it will give you an insight into what is available. By becoming a member of any of these organisations you can stay up to date with trends and information specific to your specialist discipline. It is also a great support network and another avenue to open more doors for you.

Whatever stage you are at in your career you can also join my Hospitality Superheroes Facebook group. This is a support group on Facebook that I have set up purely for people working in hospitality. It is a closed group, so feel free to ask questions and get advice from the other hospitality superhero members. You can join the group on this link:

www.facebook.com/groups/hospitalitysuperheroes

When the going gets tough

I am sure you have heard the expression 'If you can't stand the heat, get out of the kitchen', a phrase that was reportedly coined by US President Harry Truman. In other words, when the pressure is too much you need to remove yourself from the situation.

As we all know, the hospitality industry has an unfortunate reputation for long hours and low pay, which is not as true these days as it may have been in the past. It is conditions such as these that can lead to stress in the workplace, although employers are much more aware of this and do look after their employees much better these days.

As you have been reading the career stories and advice given by the hospitality professionals that were interviewed, I am sure you will have noticed that many have said how hard the hospitality industry is to work in, although it is also very rewarding. It is an industry where progression can come about quickly, and therefore it is also an industry that gives great responsibility to people early on in their career. For some this can become stressful.

It is important to highlight how to recognise the signs of stress and how to combat this. A bit of stress is normal in everyday life; it is when you get overwhelmed with the pressures and you feel you are physically and emotionally crushed that it can lead to mental health issues.

The Mental Health Foundation (2016) reports that every week, one in six adults experiences a common mental health problem such as anxiety or depression and one in five adults have considered taking their own life at some point.

How to recognise stress	
Feelings	Irritable, aggressive, impatient, unable to switch off
Behaviour	Can't make decisions, constant worrying, unable to concentrate, eating too much or too little, smoking, drinking, being tearful
Physical symptoms	Muscle tension, sore eyes, sleeplessness, tiredness, headaches, chest pains, high blood pressure, indigestion, breathing problems

The above are just some of the signs. The key is to listen to your body – if you are not feeling 100%, this is your body telling you to slow down.

Tips on how to combat the signs of stress

- Take regular breaks – go outside for some fresh air, walk around the block, change the environment you are in

- Regular exercise – this should be part of your routine, to get your body moving and release the endorphins (these are the happy hormones that are released from your brain to help you feel good)

- Talk – have a chat with your colleagues or friends about how you are feeling and share any anxiety you may have

- Sleep – getting seven to eight hours' sleep regularly will help your body to heal. Put your phone on 'do not disturb' so your sleep is not interrupted

- Take up a hobby – this downtime will let you do something you enjoy and will help to focus your mind

Putting these steps into a regular routine will help you to live a more balanced lifestyle. If you feel you do not have enough hours in the day, you need to relook at your work schedule and where you could be delegating tasks to others.

If you still feel you need help with your situation, organisations such as Hospitality Action are there to help.

Hospitality Action

Hospitality Action was established in 1837, beginning life as the 'London Coffee House Keepers Association'. It has been helping people who work in the hospitality industry and find themselves in difficulty or crisis for over 180 years.

Mark Lewis, the chief executive, explains: 'We offer assistance to people in the industry in a variety of ways. Primarily we offer financial grants to people who need support to deal with an issue that has cropped up in their lives, but we also offer counselling to people.'

You may remember Mitch Collier's story in the first section of this book. At the young age of twenty-one he was diagnosed with cancer. Through the support of Hospitality Action he was able to receive counselling for this traumatic time in his life. Thankfully, he has now been given the all-clear and his life is back on track.

Hospitality Action also supports elderly people who have spent their working life in the hospitality industry. They organise lunches and afternoon teas for them to ensure they do not feel lonely or isolated as they enter their later years. They are affectionately known as their Golden Friends.

More recently, Hospitality Action set up an employee assistance programme, which offers employers a suite of benefits for hospitality employees. Their service is a proactive, fully supported, confidential scheme that provides the following services:

- Advice and help sheets on topics that include: health and wellbeing, working life, and financial matters

- Web chat and telephone helpline, 24/7, 365 days a year

- Managerial advice line

- Managed referrals

- Personal counselling – both telephone and face-to-face counselling

- Legal information and guidance

- Financial planning and debt advice

- Addiction support – expert help with alcohol, drugs, gambling or other addiction issues

- Hardship grants – where criteria are met

- Parenting helpline – topics covered include: pregnancy and birth, single parenting, shared parenting and teenage challenges

- Elder care – support and advice on caring for an older relative

- Bespoke managerial reports, employee booklets, employer's briefing document, posters and subscribers' newsletter

- Whistleblowing service – a confidential service giving employees the opportunity to report any work-related concerns to an independent third party

- Mediation

- Critical incident and trauma support

Hospitality Action should be your first point of call should you ever find yourself in a distressing situation, such as experiencing a life-changing illness, poverty, bereavement, domestic violence or loneliness.

> **Advice from Mark Lewis**: 'Hospitality is a fantastic industry to work in, and there are opportunities to build meaningful careers. But of course, as with many other workplaces, it can be hard and pressurised at times. It is important that people know that there is a safety net in play, and if they do fall upon hard times and do come across challenges or hurdles HA is there to support them.'

To find out more about Hospitality Action, see the full video here:

www.vimeo.com/273964236

Your health and wellbeing are the most important aspects of your life. There will always be work to do, but there is only one you. Look after yourself.

As I bring this book to a close, I hope you have been inspired by hearing about the career stories from our hospitality professionals in the first section of the book. You should now be fully prepared to demonstrate your 'H.O.S.P.I.T.A.L.I.T.Y.' skills, as outlined in the second section, and finally have a clearer idea of the organisations that can help you to find your niche to develop your hospitality career.

Wherever you end up, remember to enjoy what you do, work hard, play hard, share your passion for the industry and keep the art of hospitality alive. I wish you every success with your hospitality career.

GLOSSARY

Acorn Awards – Awards for those under the age of thirty working in hospitality that have been recognised as the brightest prospects. Each year thirty award winners are announced.

www.acornawards.co.uk

AICR – Stands for **the Amicale Internationale des Sous Directeurs et Chefs de Réception des Grand Hôtels,** or the **International Association for Deputy Managers and Front Office Managers of Luxury Hotels.**

www.aicrinternational.org/uk-section

Beyond Food Foundation – Social enterprise that provides catering training and work experience at the Brigade Bar and Bistro for people overcoming homelessness.

www.beyondfood.org.uk

British Institute of Innkeeping – The professional body representing individuals working across the licensed hospitality trade.

www.bii.org

Boutique Hotelier Personal Service Star Awards – Celebrates the crème de la crème of the hospitality industry, awarding individuals and teams who work tirelessly every day to give their guest the best possible experience.

www.boutiquehotelier.com

Catey Awards – The most prestigious awards in the UK hospitality industry. The Cateys showcase innovative brands and trailblazing people from across hotels, restaurants, food service, pubs and bars. Recipients are nominated, selected and awarded by the industry through *The Caterer* magazine.

www.cateys.com

Chaîne des Rôtisseurs – International Association of Gastronomy established in over eighty countries bringing together amateurs and professionals who appreciate fine cuisine.

www.chainedesrotisseurs.com

CIPD – Chartered Institute of Personnel and Development – the professional body for human resources and people development.

www.cipd.co.uk

City and Guilds – An educational organisation that sets the standards for vocational education.

www.cityandguilds.com

Craft Guild of Chefs – The leading chefs' association in the UK, which has many members worldwide.

www.craftguildofchefs.org

Food and Beverage Managers Association – Promoting the highest professional standards of management, education and recruitment in the food and beverage hospitality industry.

www.fbma-london.co.uk

HCIMA – Hotel Catering Institutional Management Association, now known as the Institute of Hospitality (see IOH).

Hospitality Action – The hospitality industry benevolent organisation that offers vital assistance to all who work, or have worked, within hospitality in the UK and who find themselves in crisis.

www.hospitalityaction.org.uk

IHSM – Institute of Hotel Security Management – The UK's leading membership organisation for hotel security professionals.

www.hotelsecuritymanagement.org

IOH – Institute of Hospitality (formerly known as the HCIMA). The international professional membership body for managers and aspiring managers who work and study in the hospitality, leisure and tourism industries.

www.instituteofhospitality.org

Les Clefs d'Or – The Golden Keys Society is a professional association of hotel concierges. Easily identifiable by the golden crossed keys on their lapels, these members are an elite fraternity, globally connected, committed to professional development and driven to setting new standards in guest service perfection.

www.lesclefsdor.org

Master Innholders – The Master Innholders was established in 1978 by the Worshipful Company of Innholders, a City of London Livery Company, in collaboration with HCIMA (now Institute of Hospitality), the industry's professional body.

www.masterinnholders.co.uk

NACC – National Association of Care Catering. A membership organisation for those working in the care catering industry. The catering may take place in residential homes or day care for people with disabilities, the elderly or young people. It also encompasses the delivery and production of fresh or frozen meals to day centres or peoples' homes.

www.thenacc.co.uk

OFQUAL – The Office of Qualifications and Examinations Regulation regulates qualifications, examinations and assessments in England.

www.gov.uk/government/organisations/ofqual

The Clink Charity – Reduces reoffending rates of ex-offenders by working in partnership with Her Majesty's Prison Service to run projects and give practical skills to prisoners to aid their rehabilitation. The Clink restaurants allow prisoners to learn, engage with the public and take their first steps towards a new life.

www.theclinkcharity.org

The Gold Service Scholarship – This award recognises the skills of front-of-house professionals and is open to anyone aged twenty to twenty-eight working full time in the hospitality industry. Her Majesty The Queen is patron of the scholarship.

www.thegoldservicescholarship.co.uk

Springboard Charity – Helps young people achieve their potential and nurtures unemployed people of any age into work. Supporting disadvantaged and underprivileged people into sustainable employment within hospitality, leisure and tourism.

http://charity.springboard.uk.net

UKBG – The United Kingdom Bar Tenders Guild, a membership organisation offering training and international competitions.

www.ukbartendersguild.co.uk/

UKHospitality – UKHospitality is the voice of UK hospitality (hotels, restaurants, caterers, pubs, clubs, service apartments, attractions and more). It was recently formed through the merger of the British Hospitality Association (BHA) and the Association of Licensed Multiple Retailers (ALMR).

www.ukhospitality.org.uk

REFERENCES AND SOURCES OF INFORMATION

British Hospitality Association (2017). 'The Economic Contribution of the UK Hospitality Industry',
https://www.ukhospitality.org.uk/page/Reports

Mental Health Foundation (2016). 'Fundamental Facts about Mental Health',
www.mentalhealth.org.uk/publications/
fundamental-facts-about-mental-health-2016

Millington, A (2017). 'Head concierges at six of the world's most exclusive hotels tell us the most extravagant things they've done for guests',
www.uk.businessinsider.com/concierges-at-6-exclusive-hotels-tell-us-about-insane-guest-demands-2017-9

Salm, L (2017). '70% of employers are snooping candidates' social media profiles',
www.careerbuilder.com/advice/social-media-survey-2017

Smart Insights (2018). 'Global Social Media Research Summary 2018',

www.smartinsights.com/social-media-marketing/
social-media-strategy/new-global-social-media-research

Walters, R (n/d). 'Robert Walters White Paper: Using Social Media in the Recruitment Process',

www.robertwalters.com/content/dam/robert-walters/
corporate/news-and-pr/files/whitepapers/using-social-me-
dia-in-the-recruitment-process.pdf

ACKNOWLEDGEMENTS

I would like to thank the hospitality professionals who have shared their career journeys with me and those who are doing outstanding work with promoting the hospitality industry through the organisations they work with.

In particular, I would like to acknowledge the contributions from:

Stuart Ball – General Manager at SoHostel

Philip Berners – Lecturer and Course Co-Ordinator at The Edge Hotel School

Andrew Boer – Principal at The Edge Hotel School

Simon Boyle – Founder of Beyond Food Foundation

Mitchell Collier – Guest Relations Manager at Le Manoir aux Quat'Saison

Sebastian Dabrowski – Chief Executive of Paperclip Solutions Ltd

Lorraine Dale – Chair of the UKHA

Peter Ducker – Chief Executive of the
Institute of Hospitality

Alex Graeme – Founder of Unique Devon Tours

Edward Griffiths – Chair of the Judges for the
Gold Service Scholarship

Mark Godfrey – Managing Director at Deer Park Hotel

Gary Hunter – Vice-Principal at Westminster
Kingsway College

Chris Jones – General Manager at Exeter Golf and
Country Club

Arun Kumar – General Manager at the
Sunborn London Yacht Hotel

Mark Lewis – CEO of Hospitality Action

Jack McCarthy – Deputy Head Concierge at
The Cavendish

Chris Moore – CEO of The Clink Charity

Anna Napora – HR Manager at The Landmark Hotel

Adele Oxberry – Managing Director at Umbrella Training

Anne Pierce – CEO of the Springboard Charity

Neel Radia – National Chair of the NACC

Grant Ridley – Chef at the Mondrion,
Sea Containers Restaurant

Rhys Richardson – Development Chef at Servest

Michael Staub – Floor Manager at the Rosewood London

Katie Young Gerald – Founder of Bespoke Textiles

Finally I would like to thank my publisher Lucy McCarraher and her wonderful team at Rethink Press, who have made it possible for me to share these stories with you.

THE AUTHOR

Monica Or MA, FIH, MCIPD

Monica's vision is 'to raise the profile of the hospitality industry so whichever hotel a guest chooses to stay in, or whichever restaurant they choose to dine at, they are taken on a unique customer service journey where the hospitality professionals they meet along the way will create memorable experiences just for them.'

Monica is available for consultancy, training and international speaking engagements. If you would like to connect with her, she can be contacted as below:

Email: monica@starqualityhospitality.co.uk

Website: www.starqualityhospitality.co.uk

LinkedIn: www.linkedin.com/in/monicaor

Twitter: @monica__or

Facebook: StarQualityHospitalityConsultancy

OTHER PUBLICATIONS

Star Quality Hospitality – The Key to a Successful Hospitality Business

If you are an independent hotelier or restaurateur wanting to know how to run an even more successful business, this book will take you on a journey of discovery as it:

- Welcomes you into the world of hospitality

- Unlocks the secrets of the business of hospitality

- Explains how customers are your lifeline, focusing on suppliers, staff and guests

- Highlights key industry trends that must be a part of your business strategy

- Shows you how to measure your business success to remain profitable

Discover the common mistakes made by hospitality owner/ managers, from business structure through to service delivery, and read a host of practical tips and checklists that can be implemented immediately to resolve them. The solutions offered will produce optimum results which will in turn increase your profitability.

This book also comes with a set of free resources – checklists and templates – that can be adapted and used in your business. To download these resources use the following link:

www.starqualityhospitality.co.uk/book-resource

Star Quality Experience – The Hotelier's Guide to Creating Memorable Guest Journeys

To create memorable guest experiences, as a hospitality professional you need to put yourself in your guests' shoes. Go on a journey with a difference, as you explore what the hotelier in the know does before even meeting their guest, the touch points during their guests' stay, and what happens after their guest leaves. This book will give you the tools you need to make this a reality:

- Find out what you need to do to ensure your guests book with you

- Work out how much you really know about your guests

- Gain insights from esteemed hoteliers on how they make their guest experiences memorable

- Get your guests to rave about you

- Follow through and implement the top tips to keep your guests coming back

The information in this book will set you apart from your competition. It will equip you with all you need to know to ensure you take every one of your guests on a journey they will remember...

This book also comes with a set of free resources – checklists and templates – that can be adapted and used in your business To download these resources use the following link:

www.starqualityhospitality.co.uk/book-resource-2

This book is also available as an online course. For hoteliers the course is 'Delivering a Star Quality Experience', and for restaurateurs there is a tailored 'Delivering a Star Quality Experience for Restaurants' course. More information on these courses is available on my website:

www.starqualityhospitality.co.uk/hospitality-courses